VOICES OF JORDAN

RANA F. SWEIS

Voices of Jordan

HURST & COMPANY, LONDON

First published in the United Kingdom in 2018 by
C. Hurst & Co. (Publishers) Ltd.,
41 Great Russell Street, London, WC1B 3PL
© Rana F. Sweis, 2018

Third impression, 2019
All rights reserved.
Printed in the United Kingdom by Bell & Bain Ltd, Glasgow

Distributed in the United States, Canada and Latin America by
Oxford University Press, 198 Madison Avenue, New York, NY 10016,
United States of America.

The right of Rana F. Sweis to be identified as the author of
this publication is asserted by her in accordance with the
Copyright, Designs and Patents Act, 1988.

A Cataloguing-in-Publication data record for this book
is available from the British Library.

ISBN: 9781787380134

This book is printed using paper from registered sustainable
and managed sources.

www.hurstpublishers.com

This book is dedicated to ordinary men and women, whose voices deserve to be heard in the corridors of power.

CONTENTS

Foreword by Abdel Karim Al-Kabariti   xi
Acknowledgements   xv

Introduction   1
1. The Art of Being: Omar Al-Abdallat   9
2. The Lady Under the Dome: Wafa Bani Mustafa   25
3. Jihad in the Family: Naser Farhan   43
4. Survivor in Exile: Amal Sawaan   59
5. The Decider: Jeries Akroush   79
6. The Rebel Reader: Lina Asaad   97
7. Nomad at Heart: Sultan Al-Maznah   113
8. Viva La Diva: Shirene Rifai   129
9. Betwixt and Between: Jamal Shultaf   141
10. Maternal Forever: Sawsan Maani   159
Epilogue   175

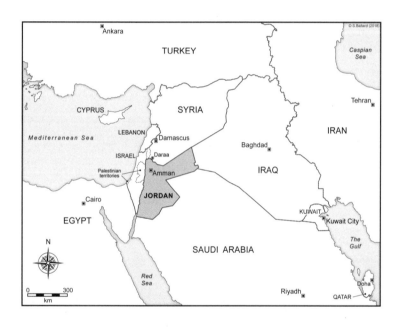

FOREWORD

The Arab world is usually perceived by the West in black and white, and recently it has mostly been seen in black. This vast and diverse region is often misunderstood, or simply viewed through the lens of its few leaders. Nowadays, the region has primarily been judged by the actions of radical ideologues who have not only targeted the West, but more often attacked Arabs themselves who do not see eye to eye with their convoluted view of the world. But this is a diverse region, in terms of ethnicity, religion and culture—a fact that has often either been brushed aside or overlooked by the outside world. The main focus of the West and of some Arab leaders has been on the stability of the region, rather than on the aspirations and different outlooks of its inhabitants.

Jordan is a microcosm of the Arab region, with its variety, frustrations, and hopes for a better future. For the region to be well understood, it must not merely be examined through the eyes of foreigners, or judged by the views of its leaders. Both its nuances and potential can only be fully recognized through the true stories of its population. Jordan embodies a diverse culture within the Arab world, and this diversity has seldom been valued or viewed as a source of strength, even within the country. Jordanians are often taught to think monolithically, whereby anything outside the mainstream is considered to be deviant or dangerous.

The lack of attention to the existing diversity in Jordan and the Arab region has suppressed minds and ideas, which has led to stagnation on many political, economic and social levels. In fact, this want of appreciation for the different thoughts and various needs of the population across the region led to the Arab revolutions in 2011. While revolutions almost never result in building stable and thriving institutions instantly, the lesson of the Arab revolutions is clear to all who want to heed it. The Arab world cannot be seen in a one-dimensional way, and the ambitions of its citizens cannot be attained without listening to the individual's voice, which represents this diversity.

Voices of Jordan successfully captures the aspirations of Jordanians from vastly varied backgrounds with a broad range of outlooks. In this powerful book, people share stories about their identity and the struggles of their country. Their voices hold the solution to understanding their way of life, for every life tells its own story. This is a story of Jordan today through the eyes of its people, and it brings their voices to life.

These voices include that of a Jordanian Christian, who represents a community of Jordanians as old as Christianity itself. Today these Christians are concerned about their status in a region more and more riddled with radical religious ideologies. The Bedouin, meanwhile, who is part of a dwindling group, tries to reconcile the traditions of his community with the demands of the modern world. The female member of parliament fights for a political role in a male-dominated culture to prove to all that she can stand on her own and assert herself in a rather conservative society. We also meet the country's non-conformers, including a cartoonist attempting to expose the challenges of his society through innovative art, and a fashion diva who constantly pushes the envelope and marches to the beat of a different drum.

Even the Jihadi, whose frustration and misguided search for a voice eventually led to violence and radicalism, typifies a segment of a generation frustrated by unmet aspirations, who have sought refuge in convoluted interpretations of the truth.

The characters in this book shed light on Jordanian and Middle Eastern lives today. Their stories provide the reader with a more comprehensive understanding of the region by giving voice to a generation no longer willing to live by the rules that their parents accepted. The characters long for better governance, a meaningful vote, economic prosperity and individual fulfilment. As they observe the political status quo around them and see no satisfying answers, they are demanding to be heard and making sure that their voices are loud enough. They are no longer satisfied with empty promises of a better life and adequate political representation. Nor are they bound by the fear factor that stifled their parents.

If the Arab world desires a transition into a pluralistic society, a different discourse is needed—one that respects diversity of ethnic origin, religion, culture, gender and outlook; one that not only addresses the challenges of the region, but begins to solve them. Only then will the young be able to resist the pull of radical, barbaric organizations like Daesh or ISIS, and only then will people of the region achieve true stability and prosperity.

I know of no better person to depict this nuanced picture than the author of this book. Rana is one of the most committed, professional, and hard-working Jordanian journalists and media researchers and has been a keen follower of developments in the region. She understands Jordanian and Arab culture as well as Western culture, and thus is in a unique position to shed light on the many people and outlooks that form Arab society.

She possesses an immense skill in weaving facts into every story she composes to present a fascinating text. The book she has produced not only accurately paints this diverse picture and evokes the changes we all need to embrace to become peace-makers, but also offers glimpses of a better tomorrow for the region.

Abdel Karim Al-Kabariti,
former prime minister of Jordan

ACKNOWLEDGEMENTS

Thank you to Omar Al-Abdallat, Wafa Bani Mustafa, Naser Farhan, Amal Sawaan, Jeries Akroush, Lina Asaad, Sultan Al-Maznah, Shirene Rifai, Jamal Shultaf, Sawsan Maani and their families for opening their homes and hearts to me. Without them, there would have been no stories to tell in this book.

I am grateful to His Excellency Abdel Karim Al-Kabariti for his kind contribution and invaluable insights into the Middle East, Jordan and this book.

I would like to thank my family: Fayez, Mona, Salameh, Rami, Dima, Beate, Mia, Haya, Taymour, Hanna and Elyas Sweis, for their support and inspiration.

I would especially like to thank Susan Wicht for believing in the idea of the book wholeheartedly and then offering her support in every way possible.

Many thanks to Salah Malkawi, the photographer for this project. His insight into Jordanian life and the images he has captured have added immense value to the words in this book. In Chicago, I would like to thank Jordyn Harrison for her photographs.

I am especially grateful to Michael Dwyer for believing in the idea and for publishing this book. Thank you to Farhaana Arefin for her wise editorial advice and feedback, as well as to the team at Hurst Publishers for all their help.

ACKNOWLEDGEMENTS

I am indebted to contributors and supporters including the European Endowment for Democracy. Their support is indicative of their belief that the stories of the people featured need to be told. I am grateful to them for their continuous support and for being unique in their commitment to human rights and freedom of expression in the Middle East. Thank you especially to Samy Lendvai-Karmout.

The first three chapters were developed thanks to supporters and friends who contributed to a crowd-funding campaign that I created in February 2016. They believed in the idea itself before I began writing, and for that, I am so grateful.

Thank you: Philippe Audi, Ahmad Alhendawi, Dina Shoman, Seif Usher, Nicolas Murat, Julia Waitring, Luay Jahshan, Natasha Tynes, Sana Samawi, Charles Tucker, Dina Baslan, Judith Van Raalten, Douglas Jones, Ramsey Day, Aoife McDonnell, Ruba Hattar, Guan Yan, Angela Perdos, Gamze Demirtola, Wendell Harris, Ciaran Devane, Muin Khoury, Nadine Mazzawi, Marius Dragomir, Lisa Ohlen Harris, Kate Wharton and Josefine Hellgren.

Thank you to the invaluable support of teachers, mentors and colleagues, especially to those who at one point took a chance on me and provided me with an opportunity to report and write: Rana Sabbagh, Osama Sharif, Carol Fletcher, Tim Sebastian, Brian Childs, Walter Paice, Michael Slackman, Marius Dergramer, Joel Campagna, Paul Van Wie, Steven Knowlton, Jerry Ulrich and Ellen Frisina.

I am grateful for the insightful conversations and wise advice from Fabian Hamilton, Sean Yom, Sami Hourani, Wendy Pearlman, Seif Usher, Curtis Ryan, Bassem Zraikat, Lana Sweiss, Anja Wehler-Schoeck, Dina Shoman, Hasan Abu Haniyeh, Wafa Abu Khadra, Tarek Osman, Marvet and Auddie Sweis, Yahia Shukier, Hiba Obeidat, Andrew Leung, Yassin Musharbash, Suha Maayah, Khaldoun Sweis, Manar Rashwani, Ahlam

ACKNOWLEDGEMENTS

Khouri, Hanan Shatnawi, Jennifer Sweis, Philip Sands, my late friend—and champion of women's rights in Jordan—Rula Quawas, and my late childhood friend Tarik Toukan.

I would like to thank my team who worked hard to help me with transcription, translation of interviews, transportation, research and for making this project possible: Rasha Algohary, Dina Baslan, Phillip O'Neil, Ruaa Ghraibeh, Rafah Sadoun, Matthew Joseph Greene, Aaron Wycoff, Ihab Muhtaseb, Sayel Hijazy, Mandie Garcia, Efeme Onaodowan and the team at Mighty Oak Grows.

Thank you to Azzam Ananzeh and my former journalism students, who taught me a lot and offered their support: Khaled Zyood, Zaid Al-Harahsheh, Arwa Omari, Nashmi Al-Sqour, Israa Qudah, Dhirar Al Shboul, Salam Akram and Abd al Rahman Hamdan.

Finally, I am grateful to the writers who continue to inspire me and who write so beautifully: Roald Dahl, e. e. cummings, Jon Lee Anderson, Anthony Shadid, Anis Chouchane, Orhan Pamuk, Ahmed Saadawi, Jhumpa Lahiri, Svetlana Alexievich and William Dalrymple.

INTRODUCTION

There was a moment during the Arab Spring between hopeful elation and the plunge into darkness. A whiff of free speech and artistic expression was being replaced by repression or worse, a descent into maelstrom. The revolutions were sparked by the tragic end of a single man, who set himself on fire to get his horrific story heard. After his death, I saw news media filled with headlines of regime change across the region and articles outlining strategic concerns, but at a time of such uncertainty, I also yearned to find the stories not being told, and the voices not being heard. I wanted to go beyond the headline news, the political analysis, and even the feature stories. This book is the story of ordinary people coping with the aftermath of the Arab Spring and its unpredictable consequences.

As a journalist, I must work within the confines of newspaper column space and word counts while always attempting to imagine the perspective of an audience that hails from afar. I have to visualize a thirty-something New Yorker walking hurriedly to the subway, or a parent in an Illinois suburb driving her kids to soccer or ballet, or a French couple in a café in Paris sitting and drinking espresso. Therefore, I ask myself two main questions before I begin working on any story: Would they read this? Why should they care? I noticed it was always the interviews and the

1

voices of the people—voters, refugees, officials, analysts, shop-keepers, activists and others—that made the greatest impact.

Living in the United States for over six years and visiting the United Kingdom in the past few years inspired me to write this book. When I attended Hofstra University in New York eighteen years ago, it seemed like I was one of only a handful of Arabs on campus. Professors, students, neighbours and shopkeepers would ask me about what life was like in the Middle East. The questions intensified after the 11 September 2001 attacks and America's involvement in the Iraq war in 2003. Later, when I lived in Washington, DC, the same questions would come up again.

As a Jordanian, the Middle East to me is much more than just another day of tragic news headlines. Jordan is a microcosm of Middle Eastern cultures and faiths. The country faces the same social and structural challenges that the rest of the region will have to tackle once the current spate of civil conflicts is over—securing meaningful employment for the youth, encouraging female and minority participation in politics, and integrating refugees into society. My cast of ten individuals, ranging from a political cartoonist to a Syrian refugee, a Jihadist to a female parliamentarian, bring the reader closer to understanding the people in the Middle East. All of them have been impacted by the Arab Spring and its aftermath, while living in a country surrounded on all sides by war and conflict. Yet Jordan stands out as a place where most personal stories are not marked by the kind of violent drama that punctuates international coverage of the region.

The story of a country or region cannot be told through the life of just one person, or as a memoir, but requires an entire choir of voices. The stories in this book are not entirely separate from each other; they are more like conversations taking place in different rooms of the same building. They are underpinned by similar contours and features, even if views and perspectives change.

INTRODUCTION

I was fortunate enough to be able to enter each room and to listen, to question, to observe. In every story the characters are having conversations in the street, at home or at work. They reflect on their own lives, the decisions they make and the region they live in, revealing the country's everyday realities. For Westerners, the daily struggles of these characters and their pursuit of economic and personal fulfilment may seem familiar. I wanted to pull back the curtain on a misunderstood region and paint the story of how different characters, not unlike their counterparts the world over, cope with the hardship, disadvantage and consequences of decades of war.

Although my main aim was to write for readers who live outside the region, the fact is that Jordanian lives do not often overlap, leaving us in the dark about each other. We Jordanians are not, in fact, having these conversations with each other. This was stated by two characters in the book: the Bedouin, Sultan, and the parliamentarian, Wafa. As I progressed with the interviews, I started to see their point. We may live in the same building, but we do not necessarily know who is living next door.

Still, Jordanians from different parts of society and outlooks share so much, even from the twin extremes of a fashionista living among the privileged class of West Amman who seeks to put her country on the map in world-famous fashion shows, to the young religious extremist struggling to carve out an existence in the harsh conditions of a northern Jordanian town. Ultimately both voices are striving to understand how they fit in a rapidly changing region and a modern state, with high aspirations for themselves and their families.

The collection of stories includes interviews and visits that span over two years, masterfully brought to life by Salah Malkawi's photographs. Ordinary people like homemakers or Syrian refugees are seldom asked to put their stories on the record. Despite people's cherished secrets and their need to keep up appearances, they also long to share their stories with the world. Perhaps they want to be remembered, but mostly they want to be heard. The people I spoke to may or may not be considered 'successful' by others' standards, yet they all embody the courage, pain and dreams of the wider society.

Surprisingly, as a woman I had more access both to people and to places. For Naser and Fayez, the Salafis, I was perceived as non-threatening. I could often speak to all members of a family, whereas if I were a man, this would not have been possible. Sometimes it was a simple gesture that made characters talk— silence, a passing joke, a court document.

Salah the photographer and I would often work separately. This was a deliberate choice. When I first met Amal, the Syrian refugee, I was with Salah. When he left, she took off her hijab and *thobe*, or long dress, lit a cigarette, tied her hair back in a ponytail and said, 'Okay, now we can talk more freely,' as if she were not being interviewed.

Interviews were usually conducted over several months, some-times years, and, of course, there were challenges along the way: no-shows, delays, cancellations, broken promises. Both the Bedouin and the Jihadi characters refused to let the women in their families be photographed. Sometimes interviews were inter-rupted, by the chattering of rats, or emotional tears, or the sounds and demands of everyday life—traffic, tending to chil-dren, phone calls. There were days when my interviewees did not want the meeting to end, so I stayed for five or even six hours.

I attempt to shine a light not only on the lives of these people, but also on the impact of modernization on an ancient but urbanizing culture. In the past few decades, regional conflicts and technology have altered Jordan, in terms of infrastructure, but also in a deeper and more personal sense for the people living there. It has created paradoxes: fear and excitement, opportuni-ties and divisions. The reverberations of war in neighbouring countries have been felt both by individuals and by society. Many live in apprehension of what might come next.

Bordered by Syria in the north, Iraq to the east, Saudi Arabia to the south, and Palestine and Israel to the west, Jordan sits in a tough and uncertain neighbourhood. And although most Jordanians are Arabs, there are also small communities of Circassians, Armenians, and Kurds. Since the 1950s, the population has increased tremendously—more than seven times over—because of natural growth and immigration resulting from conflicts in neighbouring countries.

Jordan is a Muslim-majority country, with over 90 per cent of the population following Sunni Islam while a small minority identify as Shia. Christians make up nearly 3 per cent of the country's inhabitants, and are mostly Greek Orthodox or Catholic. There are also small numbers of Baha'is and Armenian Christians. Jordan's image internationally is one of moderation and tolerance in the eyes of Westerners, who might be familiar with the country's well-known king and queen, or travel as tourists to visit the Dead Sea, Petra and Jerash. This perception of Jordan's openness is mostly correct, even though its population primarily consists of those who sit more comfortably with a rather conservative worldview.

Traditionalists continue to obstruct women's rights in the Arab world, including in the political sphere. I met Wafa Bani Mustafa, who at thirty-one years old became the youngest member of Jordan's parliament, serving as one of the country's few women representatives. Wafa's story encapsulates one of the themes familiar to the wider Arab world, as nations move toward reducing women's inequality in politics and society following the Arab Spring.

Young Jordanians feel split between family obligations and their newfound individualism and ambition. Lina Asaad offers a glimpse into her life as a Jordanian teenager through the internet and social media, tools that were used during the Arab uprisings as a means of collective activism, to reconcile increasingly complex regional developments with globalization.

Amal Sawaan's harrowing journey from Syria to the desert border of Jordan begins with a happy childhood, a heart-breaking love story, and then the horrific day when war arrived. Displaced nine times, she depicts the story of civilians caught up in the brutal civil war and of life in Jordan as a Syrian refugee.

Jordan is just over the size of Scotland, and has a population of over 9 million people, nearly half of whom live in the capital, Amman. Much of even that figure comes from refugee influxes—well over half a million since the start of the Syrian conflict in 2011. While so many have entered Jordan to find a new life, others depart to seek a better one. Jamal Shultaf, a Jordanian, left his homeland behind as economic prospects were failing him. He wants a more hopeful future for his children. The country is largely economically dependent on its neighbourhood and as a result has sustained prolonged economic stagnation. In the wake of the Arab Spring, Jordan's vital trade routes with Syria and Iraq were closed and regional instability turned some investors away. Jamal chose to settle in the suburbs of Illinois, searching for the American dream.

Jordan is home to five UNESCO World Heritage sites, including the ancient city of Petra and the site where Jesus was baptized. With an increasing amount of attention in Hollywood focused on the Middle East, Jordan offers safety and a wide choice of landscapes. Its rich cultural and historical environment has long been a benefit to its nascent film industry. Scenes from *Indiana Jones*, *Lawrence of Arabia*, *The Martian*, and 2016 Oscar nominee *Theeb* were all filmed at various Jordanian locations, including in Wadi Rum, where Sultan Al-Maznah, a young soldier and Bedouin lives.

The Arab Spring began as a people's revolution. Mass protests in Tunisia quickly toppled a president, and spread across the region. There was a belief that the 'street' could finally have sufficient voice and that Arab leadership would be forced to listen. That dream eventually died, most grotesquely on the war-torn streets of Syria's cities, or in the end of liberal aspirations in Egypt and the return to military dictatorship.

The underlying conditions forcing a desire for change have not gone away, whether grounded in economic frustration, political dislocation or social exclusion. Arguably, the challenges facing the region are worse now at the end of the decade than they were at the beginning, and there is little sign that governments can deliver coherent solutions that will satisfy the fundamental requirements of their people.

Mohamed Bouazizi, the street vendor in Tunisia who set himself on fire in 2010, changed a region, for better or for worse. Seven years later, thousands of Moroccans took to the streets to protest the death of a fish-seller, Mouhcine Fikri, who was crushed by a garbage truck. Their sense of disillusionment, but also of hope, resonates most strongly in the individual voices that we hear in refugee camps and cafés, filled with unemployed youth, or, indeed, with mothers, Bedouins, and artists.

1

THE ART OF BEING

OMAR AL-ABDALLAT

Cars rumbled over the countless cobblestones of Rainbow Street—the capital's oldest quarter, home to the riches of the city's heritage, its art galleries, street markets and the Rainbow Art House Theatre. More recently, the area has been dotted with collective spaces like Makan Café, where Omar Al-Abdallat was speaking to an audience, making a poignant case for the power of cartoons. 'Bart Simpson,' he told me afterwards, 'is more important to the world than any Arab leader.'

Omar once described his art to me as 'simple in terms of drawing but deep in meaning.' His bold, single lines and bright colours disguise more intricate details—a thorn on a chair, or an emblem on a dictator's hat. I was already familiar with his cartoons and animated videos, mostly through social media.

Omar taps into rising political and social trends, and young Jordanians make up the bulk of his audience. The Arab Spring, demonstrations that originated in Tunisia in December of 2010 and quickly spread to other Arab countries, inspired him to create a character called the Za'eem, or leader. The Za'eem wears a large beret hat, a pale blue military uniform, and a thick black moustache. He represents autocracy, corruption, and repression in the Arab world. 'He is more of a silent character,' Omar explained. 'Sometimes I use few words, or simple ones, through which I try to ridicule the Arab way of managing things.'

The Middle East today is reeling from the effects of the Arab Spring. Dictators are ruling once again, and civil wars have erupted across the Arab world. While it lasted, though, the wave of protests across the Middle East inspired forms of artistic expression and broke through the decades of self-censorship and fear that plague repressive societies.

Artists shed their fear, blatantly calling into question policies and politicians. Theatrical plays, films, rap songs, and cartoons were born as a result of the Arab Spring. They became an integral part of the changing landscape of the Middle East.

When I first met Omar—who is tall, bald, and maintains a stubble beard—his life, as he described it, seemed to be falling apart. Until recently, Omar had been sitting behind a desk, working for multinational companies as an artist and graphic designer. At thirty-eight years old, he had resigned from the last company he worked for and seemed to be on a journey of self-discovery, questioning everything he had learned, the places he visited, and the people he knew. There were questions, but there were also 'little lost battles'—delays, doubts, bad deals—that left the father of two sleepless at night.

'It was liberating but also terrifying,' he said of leaving his previous job. 'It's like someone throws you into the abyss and then says, "find the light, find your way."'

He questioned everything, it seemed, except his constant need to draw and to create. He drew every day, and every day he tirelessly pursued an idea or created a new one: a fresh character, a children's book, a new sketch. Whenever I visited Omar, whether at home or at his office, I would find his notebooks next to the computer crammed either with figures and text or with shapes. Pencil lines filled the pages, as if they were about to spill off and extend onto the table. At the time, Omar was focused on creating a new cartoon character, Sehes.

Sehes is a young man with dark hair streaked blue, two scars on his forehead, a large nose, and pink puffy lips. For Omar, Sehes represents a generation of intelligent, young, unemployed Arabs whose hopes and dreams are dashed because of their harsh environment but who use sarcasm as a way to deal with their uncertain future. Sehes ends up working as a bus driver or selling corn from a cart on the street. 'He is smart,' Omar told me. 'He just didn't find the right environment or the right education to develop his talents.'

The Arab Spring, one can argue, was brought on by a multitude of factors—political, social and economic. Jordan, like Morocco, was able to manage the Arab Spring because of limited demonstrations, fewer demands, and general support for the monarchy. Still, the largest protest took place in Amman on 13 November 2012, following a government decision to reduce fuel subsidies, effectively leading to a 14 per cent increase in the price of fuel at the pump and an increase of more than 50 per cent in cooking gas prices.

In many parts of the country, joblessness amongst the youth feels like a social plague. It stems partly from a gap between the educational system and current job market requirements. The educational curricula are antiquated, and have hardly been reformed. They are government-led and unresponsive to the needs of a growing private sector. Similarly to other countries in the Middle East, Jordan suffers from a high rate of youth unemployment. More than 70 per cent of the population is under thirty years old, and nearly a quarter of those are between the ages of fifteen and twenty-four.

I met Omar one balmy evening at a cartoon exhibition in a café in Jabal Al-Weibdeh, an old district of Amman known for its art galleries, old stones, and dusty pine trees. We sat at a small table at the edge of the café's patio overlooking a busy street. Salesmen stood outside their small shops, smoking and sipping mint tea. Omar was exhibiting a few of his cartoons, including a controversial one with the word Disney superimposed on the United Nations logo. In the lower left-hand corner of the cartoon stood Mickey Mouse, smiling, his hands on his hips. 'Political decisions are made at the UN but there is no real action on the ground,' he explained to me as he pointed at the framed cartoon. 'The UN is a playground like Disneyland.'

As we chatted, a number of designers, painters, and cartoonists who knew Omar pulled up some chairs and sat down next to us, puffing away on their cigarettes as they discussed art and digitization. One of the most popular local cartoonists in Jordan, Emad Hajjaj, was there, and I asked him where he was publishing his work. 'The newspaper, as we know it, is history,' he told me, raising his hands in the air before announcing, 'My work is online.'

When I went home, I checked Emad's Facebook page. Although his posts are not always relevant to his work, he had over 1 million fans. Artists today clearly have more followers and more direct interaction with those followers than they would through more traditional media outlets, but some artists are still struggling to capitalize on this financially. Meanwhile, Jordan's youth have proved adept at utilizing social media and mobile applications, which have become the preferred platforms of critics, supporters, commentators, and policymakers. About 5 million Jordanians use Facebook, and more than 3 million use the voice and chat mobile application WhatsApp.

Omar explained that working with these new media platforms had helped him create a new method of drawing, simpler in meaning and message so that it could be circulated and shared. Emad Hajjaj, who many would agree has opened the door for the profession to flourish in Jordan, is famous for his accurate depiction of daily Jordanian society through his detailed drawings of objects: familiar tiny items found in Jordanian households, like a portable heater and pink slippers, or on the desk of a typical bureaucrat, like cigarettes and black stamps. Omar considers Hajjaj a colleague and a friend, but also felt that it was important for him to create something unique, that set him apart, especially with the pace of technological change and rising competition from other Arab cartoonists in the Middle East.

As much as Omar's art appeals to his online audience, it has also landed him in trouble. Government officials, left-leaning and conservative quarters, tribesmen, and nationalists have all criticized him for portraying them. Shortly after the cartoonist's resignation from his former job, he met with some companies who revealed they would only strike a deal with his budding enterprise if he stopped drawing political cartoons.

'People fear freedom,' Omar messaged me on Facebook one day. 'People perceive freedom as perversion, as rebellion, but on the contrary it could mean the freedom to be more affectionate, the freedom to be more innovative.'

When he posted sarcastic comments on Facebook about the rising levels of unemployment in Jordan, he received a message from a young man, who did not identify himself, 'encouraging' him not to speak about politics anymore and to refrain from addressing social problems. But this did not deter him, and he told me:

> When someone tells me to stop speaking out or threatens me, I feel that by continuing to draw, I am not letting down the other artists who struggled before me. I will not let cartoons merely be pictures with little or no value. I want the cartoons to disturb others and reveal corrupt practices. I want it to be like a scream that echoes and reverberates for a long time. Still, sometimes, I wonder if, by choosing this path, I am being unfair to myself and to my family; I have dragged them into this profession and into this world. But this is me, and I cannot change.

When I first visited Omar at home to meet his family, he was waiting for me outside on a quiet, car-lined road. He lives with his wife and two children in an apartment, surrounded by other chalky white apartment blocks, next to a mosque in an upper-middle-class neighbourhood called Shmeisani that lies northwest of downtown in Amman. Long before malls, traffic jams, and skyscrapers had emerged there, teenagers growing up in the 1980s and 1990s would flock to the ice cream parlour, the popular pizza joint, and the VHS rental shop to while away their afternoons. Over the years Shmeisani has become the financial hub of the capital, with large bank headquarters standing like shadows in the streets.

Omar quickly apologized for the broken elevator in the building, and led me up several flights of stairs and through a hallway into a guest living room area. His wife, Sawsan, welcomed us with a soft smile, offering us blueberry muffins and strong coffee in floral ceramic cups.

The dining table was covered with books and a large computer screen. The books were all spread out, and I noticed Dr Seuss' *Fox in Socks* on the edge of the table. Books, like foreign films and his travel experiences, have influenced Omar—or at least they found their way into the many conversations we had. 'Sweden changed my life,' he told me over and over again each time we met. 'Portugal changed my life.'

In April 2015, Omar was invited to speak in Portugal at an influential TEDxPorto event, a platform that hosts videos from expert speakers. The title of the talk was 'Cartoonist and the Beast', and he began with a self-deprecating joke about being a Muslim:

> I'm going to be honest. When I first got the invitation, I was worried because they were searching for a 'Muslim' cartoonist. I said why do they want a Muslim cartoonist and why me? Am I wanted? Did I kill anybody lately? Are they going to arrest me as soon as I arrive in

THE ART OF BEING: OMAR AL-ABDALLAT

Porto? Welcome Mr Omar ... so you thought you were going to give a speech. Ha. Very funny ...

The audience laughed.

Sawsan and Omar first met at an advertising agency. 'He was a graphic designer, I was a copywriter. He knew how to tell a story,' recalled Sawsan, who is two years younger than Omar. 'We talked and laughed a lot when we were at work.' Omar described Sawsan as funny, outgoing, and optimistic. 'I didn't know how to talk to girls, but when I wasn't with her, I missed talking to her.'

As we drank sage tea, eight-year-old Adnan sat listening. His younger sister, Leen, pulled out Hello Kitty toys from a sack and then opened a small cup of chocolate pudding. Adnan was on the swim team and was happy to slip quickly into his room and come back to show off his eight school medals. Adnan also remembered attending his father's first solo exhibition in 2014, but confessed that he is not interested in art.

Although Sawsan supports Omar in his career decisions, she admitted that she grew more concerned when he left his job. 'Omar is sensitive, he has to work, he has to produce to feel he has done well,' she explained. 'He is at his best when he is productive, and so I was worried that there would be this emptiness and uncertainty that would make him feel low.' She said her fears came true when Omar, who quit smoking at the same time he left the company, became moody and quick to anger, and would stay up all night drawing.

Sawsan considers herself socially and religiously conservative—more conservative than Omar. She did not wear a hijab when she was younger but began wearing it after attending Quran classes, where she became more convinced that it was important for her to do so. She also admitted that her sisters had put pressure on her when she was younger. Omar remembers spending many hours at the mosque in his early youth and said that when he married Sawsan he was more religious than he is today. He still fasts during Ramadan, a month when Muslims across the world give up food and drink from dawn to dusk, focus on prayer, and give to charity.

Omar occasionally attends Friday prayers as well, but it was only more recently that he cautiously began to raise some questions and strike up conversations with friends and relatives about religion. He told me that he had even lost some childhood friends, including one who became a Salafi—a member of an ultra-conservative Islamic movement.

When I asked him how he sees the role of religion in his life, he answered as if he had been thinking long and hard about the question:

> Above all else now, I believe in humanity. I am on the side of religion but it has to embody universal human values. We need to revise texts that conflict with human rights. I believe in the core religious values, justice and humility, but I encourage speech that emphasizes citizenship, that focuses on love and accepting the other, because we are partners in this country. It is best to use speech that will serve humanity, speech that benefits mankind, about healing, about technology and about anything else that brings us closer to the core values of our religion.

Born in London and raised in Amman, Omar is one of five siblings. He was shy as a boy but later grew into the role of class clown. Although he did not excel academically, his talent in art was obvious early on to his mother, originally from Syria, who began painting later in her life, and his father, a prominent Jordanian military neurologist.

When the family went through a hard time financially and his brother suffered from health problems, Omar felt it was his role to entertain them and keep his siblings and parents smiling. He imitated former leaders and television personalities. When I visited his parents' home, his mother asked him to do an impersonation of an Arab leader and he complied. The room filled with laughter. I told his mother that some people might say that Omar's weakness is that he cares too much about what other people think. She looked surprised, even a bit defensive. 'That's not true,' she said. 'Who told you that? Who said that?'

Still, in February, Omar sent me a message on Facebook:

> I go to sleep and wake up in the morning thinking how ever since I began drawing cartoons, my role was to defend the rights of people and during the Arab Spring I stood by those fighting for freedom of expression and gave them everything I had. The person who I treated unjustly is myself. I thought of others at the expense of my family, at the expense of my dreams and goals. So I want to fight for my rights now.

His mother took me on a tour of their home and showed me some of her own paintings as well. She remembered how, as a child, her son used single lines, never going over the same line twice. He gave the drawings to other children to colour in, she recalled. But for a prominent neurologist like his father and for his large extended family, being an artist was shunned. 'My father supported my decisions later on, but until today people ask me only one thing,' Omar told me in front of his parents. 'What you do, does it put bread on the table?' It is a humiliating question in a predominantly patriarchal society.

Omar told me privately that his father, Adnan, wished that at least one of his sons had become a doctor. I asked Adnan if he wished his son had grown up to become something else. 'Omar is an artist. Art flows through his veins.' His mother interrupted. 'He didn't really give us a chance to think of anything else. He was obsessed with art.'

Omar spent the first two years of his life in London where his father was completing his medical degree. He has never returned to visit, but has a marked affinity for Europe, as I noted in his frequent references to its life-altering effects on him. Two months after he quit his job at the start-up company, he called me to tell me that he had been invited to speak at the Arab Cartoon Festival, a forum in Belgium that brings together cartoonists from Arab countries and Europe to share their experiences. He had prepared a speech and asked me if I would look at it:

> My childhood dream was to become a cartoonist and publish my work in a newspaper so that everyone could see my work. That almost happened when I began working at a local newspaper in Amman. I had a great relationship with the editor-in-chief there, but the staff came and went and I had a new editor and things became complicated. They began banning my work. In fact, they wanted me to draw their ideas and adhere to their thoughts. My job is to be the voice of people. And so, in 2011, they fired me.

Art exhibitions and cartoons flourished in Jordan during the Arab Spring, for example, a popular theatre production called 'Al'aan Fhemtekom' (Now I Understand You), which played to full houses for several months. It was applauded by audiences, even by King Abdullah, the current king of Jordan, but Jordanian government officials criticized it. In one scene that drew much laughter, Jordanian ministers, who are appointed by the king, are chosen by a lottery raffle rather than by merit.

Omar told me that he had attended the play twice, because 'it depicted reality, our way of life.' The title of the play was taken from a speech by former Tunisian President Zine el-Abidine Ben Ali, the day before he fled to Saudi Arabia in January 2011 after weeks of increasingly violent protests against his regime. Ben Ali's statement resonated across the region, expressing as it did the immense disconnect between autocratic rulers and their citizens.

When I interviewed the lead actor of the play, Musa Hijazin, just before he went on stage, he told me that government offi-cials who attended the play would sometimes go into the hallway during the intermission and yell 'that we crossed the red lines and the play is a direct insult to them.' Still, he noted, ordinary

Jordanians told him that 'the dialogue and dark sarcasm reflects the conscience of our nation.'

For many decades, Arabs were denied a platform for expression and were in turn plagued by internal fear and self-censorship. 'It's a constant battle not to lose the fight for more freedom,' Jumana Ghunaimat, then editor-in-chief of the daily *Al Ghad* newspaper in Jordan, told me when I interviewed her about freedom of expression and the Arab Spring. According to Omar, 'Freedom of expression has regressed tremendously, whether indirectly or directly. It has even led to imprisonment.'

From Qatar to Tunisia, poets, musicians, and bloggers who dared to speak out have been imprisoned since the revolutions. Many journalists and academics in Jordan lament the closing of the narrow window during the Arab Spring when an internal barrier of fear was lifted, and feel that the political climate has since taken an ominous turn as extremism, terrorism, civil wars, autocracy, and economic disintegration continue to plague the region.

I recall how the 2006 bombing of the Al-Askari Mosque in the Iraqi city of Samarra fuelled the civil war and forced many Iraqis to flee their homes. Since independence from Britain in 1946, Jordan has provided shelter to various waves of refugees fleeing Middle East conflicts, including Palestinians, Iraqis, and more recently Syrians. Unlike the current influx of Syrian refugees, many of whom hail from rural areas and are poor, Iraqis who arrived in the country during the First and Second Persian Gulf Wars were from Baghdad and were either wealthy or middle-class.

I met Baghdadi professors, politicians, photographers, and journalists who came to Amman to register as refugees. Another group of Iraqis—artists, actors, and designers who fled war or the financial and trade embargo imposed by the United Nations on former President Saddam Hussein in the 1990s—also found refuge in Jordan. They continue to shake up the art scene, bringing depth and experimentation. 'They raised the bar,' said Omar, 'whether as instructors or art critics, or through the artwork they have exhibited.'

The Iraqi refugee artist Saddam Jumaily is just one example. When I asked Omar and Mohammed Afefa, an award-winning Palestinian artist living in Jordan, to put me in touch with a talented Iraqi artist in Jordan, they both recommended I speak with Saddam. Saddam holds a UN refugee agency card, officially confirming his status as a refugee. He and his wife came to Jordan in 2010 and share a tiny, shabby apartment. At the end of a short, narrow hallway, his paintings were stacked in rows in a small, bright room.

Jordan has provided safety for Saddam from the violence, extremism, and harassment he endured as an art professor in the southern Iraqi port city of Basra. However, the artistic challenges endure. Although galleries and exhibitions have sprung up over the years, the art scene continues to target a niche audience in Amman. When I met Saddam, he was struggling financially. He admitted that most art galleries in Jordan refused to display some of his pieces because they were deemed too controversial, too unusual, too deep, and not marketable enough, leaving him anxiously waiting to be resettled in another country.

Whenever I spoke with exiled artists in Jordan, it amazed me that the country was sitting, for the most part, on an untapped goldmine of talent and artistic expression. Despite my feelings of frustration, I would find respite in occasional exciting announcements. A prominent art gallery in Amman, Dar Al-Anda, exhibited and promoted Saddam's mixed media artwork 'Inkography' in February 2017. I also saw three rolled up containers in Saddam's apartment that he mentioned he was shipping to America. A scholar rescue fund, helping refugee students and scholars in the region, was teaming up with the famous Christie's auction house in New York to display some of his art. 'Art records history,' he told me, as he showed me his paintings. 'I want people to decide for themselves what they see.'

Wherever I went in Jordan, mothers, refugees, public school children, and government officials recognized or identified with the characters in Omar's art. But as much as Sehes represented the realities experienced by many young people in Jordan, for Omar the character denoted a new chapter in life. In many ways, creating Sehes at a moment of personal uncertainty was Omar's salvation.

Three months after we first met at the café, Omar rented an office space at the King Hussein Business Park, which houses companies such as Microsoft, LG, and Hewlett Packard, and offers information and communications technology (ICT) infrastructure. Omar relocated his large computer, drawing pad, and books to the new office space, and pinned posters of Nelson Mandela, Star Wars, and other sources of inspiration to the walls.

The period of uncertainty in Omar's career bred creativity and new development. Six months after our initial meeting, Omar sent me an invitation to a press conference. He had teamed up with a local gaming start-up and was launching two mobile applications—a trivia game that featured his cartoons in augmented reality, and another of noughts and crosses with Sehes. He was coming to terms with establishing his own venture. 'I want people to know that art is worthy; it has an impact.'

As Omar was presenting the mobile apps to the press, I remembered something he had told me when I visited his parents:

> As an artist I know now I must not be a subordinate to a company because I will end up a slave to its ambitions, a slave to the dreams of its investors. And you mustn't be a slave. An intellectual must always be developing himself or herself; he or she has to be ahead of the game. He or she is the light, trying to shed light on society and where it is heading, where it should be heading.

A combination of regional instability, archaic bureaucracy, and unemployment in Jordan has led to a sense of apathy among

Jordanians. Omar draws on this in his cartoons. In one scene, Sehes sits at a desk surrounded by a small coffee cup, a stamp, and an animal character: Sous, which means 'chick' in Arabic. In front of him looms a mighty maze, symbolizing the complex paperwork of bureaucracy in Jordan. From his desk, Sehes is trying to navigate the maze's twists and turns to reach the finish line. Above the picture are the words: 'Dear reader, please try to help Sehes complete the paperwork.'

Occasionally there were days when, out of frustration, Omar flirted with the idea of leaving Jordan to pursue his profession elsewhere. I always wondered if he really would. The more I examined his cartoons, the more I realized that in many ways a country's identity is embodied by its political cartoonists. They hold up a mirror to society and government officials and force them to stare into their own reflection.

For decades the controversial Syrian cartoonist Ali Farzat had been depicting the mismatch between official rhetoric and what happens on the ground in the Arab world. Near the beginning of the Syrian conflict, he was forced out of his car and beaten by security officials, who notably broke his hands, according to a report by the BBC.

Violence against cartoonists and artists, however, is nothing new. Naji Al-Ali, a Palestinian cartoonist who was known to have reflected Arab and specifically Palestinian public opinion, was shot in 1987 outside an Arab newspaper in London for which he drew. The incident highlights the real dangers cartoonists face, but is also a testament to their influence.

When Omar returned from Belgium, we met at a busy café one mid-summer afternoon. Even though I was busy writing or glancing at the menu, it was hard to miss Omar's entrance—at six foot three, he was often the tallest person in the room. He was wearing a polo shirt, in his usual style.

When people came up to him to greet him—a radio journalist, a teenager, an elderly man—he would pause our conversation mid-sentence to speak with them. When they left, he sat back down and pulled out his cell phone. He scrolled through pictures he had taken during his trip and narrated the story behind each photo. He showed a picture of a building in Belgium, once the home of the late Flemish architect and artist Jozef Schellekens, which has now been converted into both a museum and a living space for artists. 'It was so inspiring,' said Omar, who resided there briefly. 'It's a different world, where art is a constant topic of conversation, and I felt they appreciated our profession.' The speech he delivered at the festival was his first opportunity outside of Jordan to present himself as an entrepreneur.

Only a few days after returning from Belgium, Omar excitedly shared an email he received from the ambassador of United Sketches, an international association for freedom of expression and cartoonists including those living in exile.

Dear Omar,

I have the pleasure to invite you to the following artist-in-residency at the Cartoonists' museum in Krems, Austria, as part of the international AIR Residencies-network. I met the museum's director to present him with a selection of cartoonists from the Arab world, and he chose your work. This residency is part of the museum's international outreach, which they wish to strengthen at the Cartoonists' museum in Krems, Austria ...

Omar confessed that it would be difficult to be away from his children, but was ecstatic about the opportunity. His savvy use of social media had also brought him a new opportunity to create dozens of Arabic emojis for a start-up company based in the United States.

Omar also shares what he has learned from his experiences by organising workshops for children and young adults across the country. He invites experts to the sessions to raise the young people's awareness of their legal rights, and helps them to build their self-confidence. Afterwards, they learn about art. 'Everything I wish I knew when I was younger, I try to pass on.'

On the same day he told me this, Omar published a funny cartoon about the parliamentary election process that was only six weeks away. The headline of the cartoon reads: 'Parliamentary elections are at our doorstep.' In it, Sehes stands in a backlit doorway, posing as a candidate and casting a long, dark shadow. He is carrying a big tray of *mansaf*, the traditional Jordanian dish of rice, pine nuts, meat, and yoghurt. Sous, meanwhile, peeks out from behind the door, wearing a chef's hat and bearing *kunafah*, a rich Middle Eastern dessert made of cheese, topped with shredded dough, sprinkled with pistachios, and doused in sweet syrup, and served at special events. The message: food for votes. The cartoon received nearly 300 likes on Instagram.

Omar's life was changing, and in so many ways, so was the region around him. One summer afternoon, Omar posted the cover photo of the children's book he began working on when we first met. 'I have days where I feel optimistic but there are also days when I feel stuck or have doubts,' he explained. 'Beginnings are always hard but you keep hoping things will turn out alright.'

2

THE LADY UNDER THE DOME

WAFA BANI MUSTAFA

From the hallway in parliament, I could hear the smile in Wafa's voice. I had just passed a line of Jordanian policemen, showing my identification card to one of them who stepped forward and slid open part of the gate, letting me into the octagonal building.

The shape of Jordan's parliamentary edifice and its repeated arches are inspired by the Islamic architecture of the Dome of the Rock in Jerusalem. The building was designed by renowned architect Rasem Badran and constructed in 1980 near downtown Amman. It houses pale-white-coloured offices behind its monumental façade, dotted with hollow bricks and glass windows.

Wafa rushed into her office, still wearing her sunglasses, an orange hijab wrapped around her hair. One phone was nestled against her ear, while she held another in her right hand. A large black handbag slowly slid, mid-conversation, from her elbow to the crook of her long arm, settling on her desk.

Tall and with brown doe eyes, Wafa never struck me as a restless person, but the pace of being productive seemed to define her being. In 2010, at the age of thirty-one, she became the country's youngest member of parliament. She had won her seat partly because of a quota system promoting reserved gender-specific seats in the lower house. After serving for a full four-year term, the budding politician competed on equal footing with male candidates in the next election, and won.

During the Arab Spring, women were seen at protests in Jordan when the government temporarily scrapped an article in the Public Assembly Law requiring consent to hold rallies. They took to the streets to call for more personal rights—like the right of Jordanian women to pass on their citizenship to their non-Jordanian spouses and children.

The first time I saw Wafa Bani Mustafa, she was apologizing to her audience for looking pale and for her hoarse voice, brought about by the flu. It was May 2015, and Wafa was speaking at a debate on education reform held in the capital. The young politician's passion translated into rapid-fire gestures, as she called for the revival of the cultural arts both in the national curriculum and outside of schools, especially in the smaller, more remote districts of the country.

From an empty, red-carpeted plot of land just off Rainbow Street, with a large screen behind her and a view of the sun setting on the city, Wafa directed questions to her audience: 'What is the main objective of our curriculum? How has it benefited our country's artists?' She was speaking at Souk Jara, or 'Outdoor Market', where Jordanians from all walks of life showcase their handicrafts, antiques, handmade soaps, woodwork and food items during the summer months.

Rainbow Street is one of the first areas in Amman to have been settled and sits atop one of Amman's seven hills, overlooking the old city below and the ancient citadel. The street was once home to Jordan's late King Talal, the reigning monarch's grandfather, is the location of the British Council, and was where the city's first private schools were established, including The

Ahliyyah School for Girls and The Bishop's School for Boys. In May 1997, the first internet café in the Middle East, Books@café, opened its doors here. Today, there are traditional coffee houses, rooftop bars, and old and new falafel shops. At the end of the narrow market, where Wafa spoke at the local debate event, there are often film screenings, shows by local bands, and other performances.

Wafa and her family come from the northern town of Jerash, a city renowned for its Roman ruins and rich archaeological sites. The local economy relies heavily on olive produce and tourism. However, just 20 miles to the north lies the border with Syria, where a civil war has been raging, a regional conflict that has all but halted the dwindling trickle of foreign tourists.

Prior to the Arab Spring of 2011, it was easy for visitors to book a package tour of three spectacular sites of the ancient world—starting at Petra, the rose-coloured rock city in southern Jordan, with a stop at the Roman ruins of Jerash, and on to Palmyra in Syria. In 2015, the extremist militant group ISIS, the so-called Islamic State, took over Palmyra. Valuable artefacts from the archaeological site were looted or destroyed before the Syrian army retook control in 2016. In December 2016, ISIS recaptured the city before they were driven out for a second time three months later by the Syrian army.

Palmyra was named by its Roman rulers in the first century AD to mean 'city of palm trees'. It has much in common with Jerash: both were crossroads of cultures in the ancient world, and both feature well-preserved colonnades and majestic Roman amphitheatres. Recent excavations indicate that Jerash has been inhabited since the Bronze Age (3200–1200 BC), leaving behind layers of antiquities from the ancient Greek, Roman, Byzantine, and Umayyad empires. Jerash once thrived as a trade hub, and the original main thoroughfare, the Cardo Maximus, is located at its centre. Visible chariot marks in the stone streets and an impressive underground drainage system hark back to the numerous rich civilizations that thrived here. For more than thirty years, since 1981, the annual Jerash Festival of Culture and Arts has played host to international artists performing on the main site. Singers, musicians, dancers, and actors from across the world converge for one month in the summer, bringing a riot of colour and melody to the city's amphitheatre.

Experts assert that no more than one quarter of the ancient city has been excavated, and that important Roman ruins probably lie under existing markets and houses. Acknowledging the recent slump in tourism, Wafa is well aware that her city needs to aspire to become a bigger cultural magnet for visitors. 'We will work hard to bring private and public investments to our city, including the building of a hotel,' she declared during her 2016 campaign speech, in the presence of close to 6,000 people.

Today, Jerash retains its rich diversity, counting more than 200,000 inhabitants. 'If you want to see all Jordanians in one place, come to Jerash,' Wafa explained at our first meeting in the parliament building. 'The population of Jerash includes Chechens, Kurds, Christians, Circassians, Palestinians, farmers, Bedouins, and others.'

In stark contrast with Jerash's lusciously green and serene vast hills, the city's downtown and main market are shabby and over-crowded. Vendor carts and fruit boxes, filled with tomatoes, radishes, and lettuce, choke the pavement and the row of small stores.

I saw Wafa in action on 14 April 2016, inside a modest office building in the centre of downtown. Nearly every Thursday, from morning until late afternoon, she receives hundreds of constituents. The vast majority of them turn to her for solutions: more national aid for a disabled son, preventing a planned road that would slice through a bakery shop, helping a patient waiting for a lung transplant. In the past, her role as the community's problem-solver was traditionally held by male elders. 'It's about that direct interaction,' mused Wafa, as she carefully examined a written complaint she had received. 'It's also in my nature to react directly to get some of these issues resolved.'

For the most part, Wafa resolves problems using her expertise and extensive network, but she also draws on her experience as a lawyer. I asked her why everyone comes to her office at the same time, and she replied:

> I feel that people in our society don't know much about one another. Yes, we joke that outside of Amman people keep an eye on each other, that it's a close-knit community, and they even meddle in other people's business, but this is all changing with urbanization. People don't know about the issues and problems affecting others anymore. Everyone thinks his or her problem is the most urgent. So I like that people are sitting with each other in this office. Many times individuals themselves conclude, 'No, you know what, my problem is not a priority, my problem is not urgent.' I like that I get them to see and feel that way. For them to come and listen to and witness the levels of injustice others are facing and the tough conditions they are enduring, that's important to me. It increases empathy. Sometimes they help each other without my involvement. I only tell them to meet at my office. It forces people to be humble. Our society is accustomed to the idea that there are leaders and elites. When one of the elite has to wait outside like everyone else, he or she may feel that it's unfair or that they are being marginalized, but the point is equality. So let the elites become aware of others and their problems. My office is open to all so they can get to know one another. I insist on that approach, even though it's exhausting because people keep interrupting; they keep talking. But it's okay, I am used to that.

That day I saw men and women of all ages. They were each waiting their turn, clutching pieces of crumpled lined notebook paper with numbers scribbled in blue ink. An elderly man stared down at the number 83 he held in his hand. The office was decorated with a Quranic tapestry in a golden frame, a large photo of the former monarch of Jordan, King Hussein, a pencil case with a faded McDonalds sticker, and books in Arabic, mostly about Jerash. Through a large window, in the hilly distance, stood the Roman ruins protected by a long fence and low walls.

Some of the people present had travelled many miles by public transport and waited for hours to see her. 'I heard she gets things done,' whispered Munifa Zaboon, a middle-aged woman who was seated across from Wafa. 'Then I met her at a wedding and I thought, "She's someone I can talk to." I am going to ask her if she can help my son re-join the army so he can get back to work. Both my husband and I are retired and we can't keep up with the expenses.'

Munifa wished to see her son support himself. Like in many other Jordanian families, her children continued to live at home, and were choosing to marry later. The average cost of marriage in Jordan is nearly $14,000, while the average monthly salary is only about $640. Traditional notions of stability are becoming harder to achieve.

When Wafa ran for office, she did so to work on legislation, but the combined lack of municipality elections in the past, inadequate budgets, and bloated bureaucracies have turned the lower house into a social services body, diverting it from being a genuine political and legislative body.

I opened this office because so many people were coming to my house seeking help. My relatives still come to my house. People come to my parents' house and they even come to my husband's family's home to find me. This is a small town, people know where I live, and they know my car. I can't hide. I should be honest with my people and solve their issues. For those who come to see me in my office, I think about the money they spend on public transport to get here and the hours they spend waiting for their turn. For some women, this is the first time they are seeking help because I am also a woman and they can talk to me. As a parliamentarian, I am supposed to focus on legislation, but most of my time is spent on social services: following up on medical cases, finding solutions to bureaucratic procedures, providing legal aid. I even had to start a small charity though sometimes I cannot afford it, but some people who come to me are in a desperate situation.

Since 1993, voting in Jordan has largely been driven by individuals' social standing rather than by their affiliation to a political party, a result of the country's enshrined tribal history and the long period during which political parties were outlawed. In 2016, a new election law was passed with an emphasis on a more proportional system meant to improve and diversify representation in parliament. Despite widespread support for her work in the community, Wafa explained how the new process would take time. Tribal allegiances remain a powerful reality in Jordanian politics.

Sometimes tribes choose a woman to represent them because they think it will guarantee them a seat in parliament. 'Our society is still patriarchal and tribal even in the political domain. Small tribes sometimes send a woman representative to run for parliament, but they still think it's their domain,' said Layla Naffa, project director at the Arab Women's Organization, a non-profit organization founded in 1970 by a group of female activists to promote equal rights in Jordan. 'Even though they choose a female representative, the idea is to stump for bread-and-butter issues rather than female empowerment. They don't really want her to represent women's rights,' explained Layla during a 2011 interview on the Arab Spring and the status of women in the region. Nevertheless, in the 2016 Jordanian parliamentary elections, an unprecedented 20 out of 130 MPs were women, marking an increase of 17 per cent in female representation since 2013.

After her day ended, Wafa offered to drive me in her modest, dusty car to meet her two children. We wove our way past double-parked vehicles, obstructed pavements, and shops with plastic toys hanging by thin ropes under neon signs. A few passers-by greeted Wafa as we approached a car park hidden between two crumbling buildings. In the passenger seat of her car, I found a pile of work papers and a copy of the Jordanian constitution.

As we inched our way out of the downtown area, I asked Wafa if we could stop by the Arch of Hadrian, an 11-metre-high gateway originally erected to honour the visit of the Roman emperor in AD 129 to the city and where many visitors begin their tour of Jerash. As she drove, Wafa was still thinking aloud about some of the requests she had received in her office. 'You remember Fatima from today?' she asked randomly. 'She is lost. The municipality is planning to build a road that will require the demolition of her house. She needs help in filing the paperwork to oppose this decision.'

We got out of the car and proceeded on foot through an indoor handicraft market. As we passed, shop owners jumped to their feet to greet the parliamentarian, shaking her hand and extending bottles of water and offers of coffee. One man hastily walked up to her and asked if she had reviewed his case. A young boy handed her one of the balloons he was selling on white plastic straws. When we finally arrived at the arched gateway, a local tour guide accompanying Italian tourists informed them of who Wafa was and they promptly asked if she would pose for photos with them. In between snaps, they asked her how many women sat in the Jordanian parliament; at the time, there were eighteen.

On her way home, Wafa called Omar, her ten-year-old son, to inquire about an exam he'd had that day at school and to find out if he and his younger brother, Haitham, were home. The boys were preparing to go to their Taekwondo class, but she asked them to wait for her to get home. Wafa's other phone, which she uses for work, started to ring, and she deliberated before eventually answering. It was someone she had met with earlier that day at her office. He wanted to let her know that he had provided the wrong number for the case he had submitted. 'People have come to rely on me as though I have all the solutions to their problems,' sighed Wafa. I was curious to know how she balances her time between family and work. She told me:

> There is no balance. Even Americans asked me the same question when I was visiting Washington, DC for a work conference. I replied that work–life balance is a lie. It doesn't exist. Sometimes work prevails and I totally forget about my family. Only on some days. Other days, I forget the whole world when I am spending time with my kids. But because I became a parliamentarian when my boys were still young, they are used to it. They definitely miss me. Sometimes they say things that pain me. For example, my eldest son, who has a sharp tongue like mine, says to me when I enter the house, 'Is this hello, hello, or is this hello, goodbye?' He says this because sometimes I just go to check on them, to make sure they are okay before I have to rush out again. It's not easy for me because I'm very attached to them. I get very emotional with my children. I may not believe in work–life balance but I believe in the quality of time I need to spend with them. I always talk to them. Of course, my husband has played a big part. Their father gives them a lot of his time and at the same time he has been extremely supportive. This is the price I have paid for becoming involved in politics at a young age.

Both phones kept ringing as Wafa drove me through her city. On a small hill nestled between pine and olive trees, she parked in front of a dusty white apartment building with green window frames, an unlocked front door leading to a dimly lit corridor. We walked up several flights of stairs before she unlocked her own front door to be greeted by her two sons, who smiled shyly. She hugged them before they scurried away to sit on the couch in the living room while Wafa made coffee in the kitchen. 'Isn't it shameful you are coming during lunchtime and all I am serving you is coffee?' she asked ruefully as she advanced with a tray of coffee and dates. 'People are surprised to know I can actually cook well.'

'We know what we want to be when we grow up,' interrupted Omar, her older son, barely concealing his pride. 'I am going to be a parliamentarian and my brother is going to be a doctor.' Haitham, who resembles his mother, nodded, and the two boys dashed to their room to change into their uniforms of heavy white cotton.

When someone asks Wafa an unanticipated or difficult question, she smiles and falls silent for a few seconds, before answering with an adage. During a local television interview, for example, a male interviewer awkwardly asked her if she thought there were any beautiful women in parliament. After berating the interviewer, she paused for a few moments, then replied: 'I don't know what you are getting at but there's a French saying: be beautiful but shut up. I don't agree with that. They shouldn't. I cannot be silent and my biggest supporter is my husband.'

Never had a woman held public office in Jerash before Wafa. It is precisely for this reason that she works all hours of the day, sometimes to the detriment of her health and at the expense of spending time with her family. The young politician also serves as a member of the Parliamentary Committee on Women and Family Affairs, which deals mainly with gender equality and social policies. She was selected to head the pan-Arab Women's Parliamentary Coalition to Combat Domestic Violence, and had been appointed as a board member at the National Centre for Human Rights.

'When you have responsibilities, you pressure yourself to make sure you succeed, don't you, sweetheart?' Wafa's mother, Samiha, told me during a campaign rally in September 2016. With every step, Wafa knows her performance is being scrutinized and women, she told me, especially from her traditional district, have a lot to prove. I asked Wafa why she chose to run for a seat in parliament when she was only thirty-one years old.

> I'll tell you why: because I was appalled at the reality that I was living in. I didn't want to continue conceding. I wanted to react. I speak

about the need for more freedoms, about fighting terrorism, about the economy and the election laws, but my priority is to fight discrimination against women. That is my cause. I was visiting the southern city of Maan a couple of days ago and called on the women there. 'Don't be fooled by those candidates that claim women make up half of society. Some female candidates themselves are fooling you when they proclaim that women are half of the society.' When those same women become members of parliament, examine who has voted against women's issues in the parliament. More often than not, it's those very same female parliamentarians, unfortunately.

Wafa was born and raised in Jerash. Her mother Samiha married Wafa's father at the age of fourteen, and they had seven daughters and four sons. Her sister's recent death from cancer has driven Wafa to prioritize medical requests she receives at her office. 'I know that I can't help everybody and I don't lie to people. I talk to them frankly. I say, "I can't, for example, provide you with a job, but if you need healthcare, I can help." If there are medical cases not covered by the public health insurance, I try to help.'

Wafa's father passed away when she was sixteen years old, leaving her mother to raise their eleven children. At her daughter's campaign launch in September 2016, Samiha wore a loose black velvet floor-length *thobe*, or long dress, that hid her body. As she sipped from an orange soda, she recalled what her husband had impressed upon her when he became gravely ill: to ensure that their daughters' education remain a top priority. She told me:

> Their father told me education would be their weapon in life. He was ahead of his time and I made sure that my daughters had the freedom to accomplish their goals and dreams. Wafa changed the way women are seen in our community and if anyone tells me a woman's place is only in the home or she has no right to speak up, I simply don't accept this argument and I'm not willing to listen to it. Ever since Wafa was a child, I remember how she was always elegant, calm, and

smart. Her school grades were high. From an early age, she displayed leadership qualities and ambition. She also played tennis frequently with her younger sister, Manar, and in school they would choose Wafa as a speaker and to lead the student council. Sometimes the price of ambition is high; we miss her at family gatherings. Sometimes her husband and boys are there but she's not. But, when I observe the crowds today who have turned out to hear her speak, I am overcome with pride and joy at the impact she is making.

In 2011, many Jordanian women and human rights advocates, including Wafa, criticized a committee responsible for drafting new amendments to the Jordanian constitution. The proposed document failed to include the principle of gender equality by barring discrimination 'on the grounds of race, language or religion', without reference to gender. The committee argued that the word 'Jordanians' compromises both men and women.

As the youngest parliamentarian at the time, Wafa showed that she cares deeply about youth issues. Jordan is now one of eight countries in the Middle East and North Africa where more women than men attend university. Yet, their education is not yielding jobs. A disparity between male and female employment levels exists in several countries in the neighbourhood, but in Jordan it is higher than the regional average.

The second time I saw Wafa was in November 2015. She was speaking at a graduation ceremony for an international programme that promoted greater political engagement amongst less advantaged women, particularly in decision-making processes and community affairs. After the young men and women presented some of their local initiatives, Wafa took to the stage. When I mentioned later that I had seen her at the event she told me she had prepared a speech but had ended up going off script.

The sight of the young audience reminded me how I was not long ago, so I needed to speak directly from the heart. I told them they should never give up and to keep fighting for their rights despite what their family and society might think. I told them that I faced many challenges but I am where I want to be now.

Two months after I witnessed Wafa's interaction with her constituents at her office, parliament was dissolved, prompting her to embark on her third election campaign. In Jordan, the king is authorized to approve amendments to the constitution, declare war, command the armed forces, and dissolve parliament. Although he also appoints the prime minister and members of the upper house of parliament, the lower house, in contrast, consists of 130 elected members, with fifteen seats reserved for women, nine for Christians and three for Circassian and Chechen minorities. In both assemblies, members serve four-year terms.

While female participation in the Jordanian parliament has increased over the past decade, it remains low relative to developed countries. On average, women hold nearly 20 per cent of parliamentary seats worldwide, according to the World Bank. In Jordan that number remained low until the 2016 elections; before then fewer than 14 per cent of seats in parliament were held by women.

Women's absence from high-profile political posts is the result of the way they are traditionally viewed in politics. Despite their appointment as judges and ministers by the king, Jordan's patriarchal and conservative culture, the argument goes, makes it difficult for women to play prominent political roles.

During the Arab Spring, women joined the protests in Egypt, Yemen, and Tunisia. However, their efforts and momentum generally have yet to be translated into leadership roles that are so vital to the future of their countries. Female representation in parliaments directly after the Arab Spring has been either absent or obsolete. In Kuwait, the 2012 parliamentary elections resulted in an all-male chamber and in 2013 only one woman was able to win a seat. During the rule of Egypt's deposed President Mohamed Morsi, women made up less than 2 per cent of the newly formed parliament. That number rose to 14.9 per cent in the 2015 elections, including fourteen female members who were directly appointed by the current president, Abdel Fattah el-Sisi. The president in Egypt appoints 5 per cent of the 596 seats in parliament.

In the months leading up to the 2016 elections, my calls and messages to Wafa went unanswered. Finally, she sent me a photo message to let me know that her campaign launch would be held on 9 September, just eleven days before the election. The public event was held on a weekend in an empty plot of land in the heart of Jerash. Wafa was running on a national list called Asalah, or nobility, which she had formed along with three male candidates. The word Asalah derives from the Arabic word for 'thoroughbred horse'—*aseel*—and so the logo for their list was a golden-brown stallion. Asalah would be running against nine other lists, so the competition was intense.

When I arrived at the campaign launch that warm, sunny afternoon, I was surprised to see thousands of cars parked and double-parked along the sides of the roads and on the hill nearby. In the sea of people I saw children cooling off with different flavoured ice lollies. Women were clutching their handbags and chatting, young men were taking selfies, and old men were reaching for their *misbahas*, or worry beads, waiting for the candidates' speeches.

As I walked around, a woman carrying pocket cards with photos of the candidates greeted me with a smile. She introduced herself as Alia, Wafa's older sister. Taking a seat next to me, she said they were expecting thousands of people to show up. She and her siblings were busy updating their sister's Facebook page and managing the numerous calls to her cell phone. In fact, when I had called Wafa a month later, it was Alia who answered.

Wafa walked up to the podium to speak, wearing a flowing traditional embroidered dress and the same orange scarf she wore the first time we met. A large Jordanian flag was draped on the side of the stage and a few men in heavy suits wearing dark glasses stood behind her as she addressed the crowd. She spoke confidently, gesturing with her hands, in her signature manner, praising the people of her town. 'You are a noble people,' she told the crowd as they cheered. 'You are the people of my beloved town whom I have served and will continue to serve. You are worthy of better services, and I promise you that. We deserve to have more investments and I promise you, we will work on that.'

Seven days later, I received a message from Manar, Wafa's youngest sister, inviting me to an all-women campaign launch. This was the second time Wafa had organized a women-only rally. There must have been a few hundred attendees. Many of the supporters were neighbours and relatives, including mothers with their children. Husbands dropped off their wives and drove off. I recalled my first meeting with Wafa at the parliament building when she had shared how important it was for her to hold such an event.

> Previously, if women attended campaigns, they would just listen. But it's like they don't exist and can't see. So I told my team that for the next elections I wouldn't have women be observers only. They said, 'Wafa, that will cost you votes from conservative men.' I replied, 'I don't care.' I will have two campaign launches. I am a woman, and I will be the first to have women come not just to eat dessert, or come with their kids and be treated like they are decoration. I refuse for them to be treated that way. So, the organizers in the team asked me what I wanted to do. I said that just as I was going to have a main launch where many men attend, I would have a launch for women. So I had a female-only campaign launch in 2013 and invited all the women of Jerash. It was a public invitation to all of them, just like all my campaign launches in the kingdom. You wouldn't imagine. I mean, I didn't cry once during my electoral campaign except on that day. I didn't even cry when I won. I only cried then, when I saw all

these women at the launch, because so many attended, thousands attended. The ushers were women. The moderators and speakers were all women.

As it turned out, the 2016 elections would prove to be challenging for Wafa, not least owing to the number of eligible candidates. Forty people, including eight women, were running on nine lists in her district. Although there was only one seat specifically reserved for a woman, female candidates could also secure a seat outside the quota. Furthermore, the new election laws meant that Wafa could no longer run as an independent candidate, so she had to choose a list to carry her. A third challenge came from the fact of running against another woman. Huda Etoom, a popular member of the conservative Muslim Brotherhood, had harnessed thousands of supporters when she copied Wafa's women-only style launch in the seclusion of her garden.

At the campaign launch, Wafa spoke mainly about her fight for women's rights in Jordan and the region, without doubt a remarkable undertaking for a little-known female politician from Jerash. For the first time, I had the nagging feeling that Wafa and her running mates were feeling the heat. Another candidate on her list shared a concern about rumours circulating on Facebook that those running on the Asalah list were campaigning more as individuals than as a group. Then Wafa chimed in: 'Please remember, each vote counts even more this time around. Please vote for all of us.' Behind her smile, her exhaustion was evident. As I was leaving, I smiled at Wafa and she greeted me. 'Your voice,' I warned. 'It's going again.' She smiled and nodded. Her sons stood next to her and posed for photos before walking around the podium.

I was covering the elections from Amman with a colleague from the *New York Times* on 20 September 2016. We saw candidates and volunteers hanging around polling centres—in front of school buildings and campaign headquarters. Voter turnout was lowest in the two largest cities, Amman and Zarqa. In smaller towns like Jerash, analysts predicted the results would be announced the following day. I kept checking various websites and media outlets, trying to find a reliable source to tell me if Wafa had won. The next day, I saw her name on the winning list. Wafa had succeeded, but unlike in the previous election, she had won the seat reserved for women. Huda Etoom, on the other hand, won by direct competition and received the third highest number of votes in her district. For the first time in its history, Jerash now had two female parliamentarians representing its citizens. Manar sent me a text: 'She won. That's it. We will have a party at sunset to celebrate.'

Although the first parliamentary session did not take place until November, or nearly two months after election results were announced, Wafa was back at work the following week. Her first public appearance was at a meeting for the pan-Arab Women's Parliamentary Coalition to Combat Domestic Violence. She was also invited to make a commencement speech at a high school graduation ceremony in her district. Later she appeared on a television show to speak about what citizens should expect from the next parliament. On Wafa's Facebook page, she posted a message to those who voted for her:

> From the bottom of my heart I would like to thank my family, my tribe and all the sons and daughters of my district of Jerash for putting their faith in me. I want to thank them for giving me the opportunity to represent them and be their voice in parliament for the third consecutive time. I will be the voice that will not be silenced when it comes to your rights and privileges. With God's will, I shall succeed.

3

JIHAD IN THE FAMILY

NASER FARHAN

The first time I met Naser Farhan, we stood silently next to each other in a narrow, poorly lit corridor. Policemen, guards, and lawyers swirled around us at the State Security Court, a special body that has jurisdiction over crimes considered harmful to Jordan's internal and external security.

Naser stood with his shoulders slumped forward, his face buried under a brown beard. I asked him if his eighteen-year-old son Fayez, who had been accused of promoting the so-called Islamic State on social media, was guilty as charged. 'He's not guilty,' Naser told me, shaking his head and leaning against the white wall.

Earlier in the day, Fayez looked out from a large black cage in the courtroom, drowning in his dreary, oversized jumpsuit. His shaved head made his delicate features even more prominent and I was struck by his youthful appearance and overconfidence.

His father and I agreed to speak later that day by phone to discuss the case further. Afterwards, the judge agreed to let me read and photocopy the charges brought against Fayez. The state-

43

ment claimed that Fayez had begun using the internet in July 2014 to share news and promote the ideas of the Islamic State, also known as ISIS or Daesh, on his Facebook page. He was also accused of sharing videos of 'operations' conducted by ISIS on Facebook and via WhatsApp. The statement mentioned that he had chanted and expressed support for the group, along with other supporters of ISIS, in a house in Zarqa, an industrial town in eastern Jordan that had become a hotbed for extremism.

In 2014, as ISIS was gaining ground and capturing territory in neighbouring Syria and Iraq, Jordan amended its anti-terrorism law, broadening the definition of terrorism to include the use of information and communication technologies to promote, support, or fund terrorist acts.

Notably, Jordan is also a member of a US-led coalition against ISIS, a position that many ordinary Jordanians once took to be meddling in other countries' affairs. However, public support for a more offensive and defensive role against ISIS took a firm hold after the Jordanian Air Force pilot Muath Al-Kasasbeh was captured and immolated by ISIS, and more recently following attacks on Jordanian soldiers and security forces in Rukban on the country's border with Syria.

It is no secret that the wars in Syria and Iraq have become a training ground for radical Jihadists from across the world. The conflicts have also lured more than 2,000 Jordanians, the vast majority of them joining either the Al-Nusra Front (also known as Al-Qaeda in Syria) or ISIS. In the past two years, Jordan has stemmed the flow of fighters by tightening its borders and detaining those who attempt to return. Many of the returnees stood trial at the State Security Court. One such case was a Jordanian who joined as a cook for Al-Nusra Front but who became disenchanted with the group only a week after arriving there and decided to return home.

I called Naser the same afternoon we first met in November 2014 and asked him if there was any progress with his son's case, and if I could visit him at home along with a photographer. He agreed, with some hesitation in his voice. I took the court document with me and we drove around his neighbourhood in the poor, central town of Russeifeh. Rows of homes were stacked on top of each other, mostly made of dusty beige slabs of concrete.

It was cold and the sky was dark, even though it was still early afternoon. An old man with thick glasses leaned on his cane as he sat in front of a small grocery store across from Naser's home. A stray cat purred next to him. All the other stores nearby were closed—most of them had worn blue shutters with signs that looked like ripped umbrellas. Random black rubbish bags, empty crisps packets, and squeezed juice cartons littered the cracked pavement. There was nothing green around—no plants, no trees, no fields.

Naser welcomed us into the small office he had built on the front porch of his home. Outside, Fayez's name was spray painted on the wall in bright red graffiti, its colour standing out against the grimness of the neighbourhood's tin roofs. Naser sat on the edge of his chair, only giving 'yes' or 'no' answers to my questions. I read the allegations against his son from the document I had obtained from the court. He looked surprised, not at the accusations but at the court papers, and then asked if he could read them.

The fifty-year-old father began to seek my advice—what would happen to his son in prison, and even after he was released? I grew silent, but Naser went on to speak for more than an hour—about his family, his neighbours, his daily life, Iraq and Syria. As he talked, we drank tea and ate dates.

Naser is a Salafi. The word *salaf* means 'predecessor', a reference to the early ages of Islam, which Salafis take to represent a bright and glorious era, during which Islamic Sharia law was properly understood, implemented, and adhered to in all spheres of society. I met with Naser regularly for nearly two years to better understand this group of people in Jordan that we only ever read or hear about. Often I noticed him wearing kohl, or eyeliner, commonly used by modern-day Salafi Muslims because it is believed to have been worn by the Prophet Muhammad. It is supposed to protect the eyes, cleanse them of harmful substances, and bestow strength and clarity.

If it were up to Salafi hard-liners like Naser, they would control the mosques, enforce strict dress codes, shut down liquor stores, and ban cultural events they deem blasphemous. One day Naser told me that when he was younger, he had sat in front of a liquor store in his neighbourhood for months, trying to persuade the owner to shut down his store and urging customers not to buy alcohol. The owner had eventually called the police and Naser had been forced to leave, but still, he thought, 'I was performing my duty.'

Mohammad Abu Rumman, one of Jordan's foremost experts on Islamic movements and author of *Ana Salafi* (I Am a Salafi), writes that even the definition of Salafi is contested within Salafi groups—between those who advocate for Salafi-Jihadism and 'traditional' Salafis. Traditional Salafism 'is conservative, academic and proselytizing. It promotes the Salafi Call and education, and it eschews political participation.' By contrast Salafi-Jihadism, writes Abu Rumman, condemns contemporary secular Arab governments as infidels and views Shias and the West as enemies, as well as any Sunni Muslims whom they consider apostates. They advocate a radical and sometimes violent approach to change. A prime example is Abu Musab Al-Zarqawi, the Jordanian man considered to be the founder of ISIS, who was the head of Al-Qaeda in Iraq until he was killed by a US airstrike in 2006. The Salafi movement evolved from the mid-1980s, following the Soviet occupation of Afghanistan in the late 1970s that saw many Arab fighters, including Jordanians, go to join the fighting.

At the age of twenty-two, Naser flew to Islamabad in Pakistan, and then to the city of Peshawar to fight in Afghanistan. 'We

1. At the age of thirty-one, Wafa Bani Mustafa became the youngest member of parliament in Jordan.

2. Wafa at home with her sons, Omar and Haitham. The two boys grew up watching their mother campaigning, working to improve conditions for her local community in Jerash, and advocating for women's rights in Jordan.

3. Wafa making a speech during a women-only campaign rally in September 2016.

4. Wafa greeting a supporter at the women's rally.

5. Omar Al-Abdallat at home with his wife Sawsan and their children.

6. Omar holding cardboard cut-outs of his characters Sehes and Sous. Sehes represents a generation of young, educated, underemployed Arabs.

7. Omar drawing one of his characters, the Za'eem, who represents autocracy, corruption, and repression in the Arab world.

8. Amal Sawaan sitting by the small propane gasoline heater around which her family congregates in winter. The same heater is used to boil tea and coffee, and sometimes serves as a stove for cooking meals.

9. Amal standing in front of trailers at the Zaatari refugee camp in Mafraq, one of the largest refugee camps in the world. Amal was displaced eight times within Syria before she finally arrived in Jordan in 2013. She lived with her family in this refugee camp for a few days.

10. Amal sitting on her bed in her home in Jordan, holding a certificate of participation in a home maintenance course.

11. Naser Farhan finds solace and hope at his local mosque, where he can often be found.

12. Naser walks down his street in the northern Jordanian town Russeifeh. Neighbours described Naser as a kind person and said they turned to him for advice in a neighbourhood that lacked community leaders.

13. Naser celebrating the wedding of his son in 2017.

14. Jeries Akroush standing with his wife Nancy on their balcony.

15. Jeries in his real estate agent's office. As a bureaucrat, Jeries finds comfort in routine and familiarity.

16. Jeries and his family at their home in the predominantly Christian town of Fuheis.

didn't know anything,' he recalled. 'We were just young men who wanted to fight for a cause and we thought this was our cause.' He didn't tell his parents where he was going and only informed them when he arrived in Pakistan. I once asked Naser's mother how she had felt when she had received the call from her son in Pakistan. The seventy-year-old put her hand on her heart and shook her head from side to side. 'I was terrified, but at the same time I wanted to be with him. I was so afraid something would happen to him.'

When Naser arrived in Peshawar, he asked about the Arab 'crowd' and was led to the other young men like him who came from Yemen and Saudi Arabia. He was also taken to a training camp where the fighters built up their physical endurance and practised using weapons: 'We trained on whatever we could get our hands on at the time, like Kalashnikovs.' After nearly three months, Naser packed his bags and returned to Jordan. 'The leaders told us we were not needed. There were already too many volunteers but at the same time there was fear about sending Arabs into battle because of the brutality they would face if they were captured by the Russians.'

Naser also became disenchanted with the splits within the groups, especially between those who wanted to wage jihad in Afghanistan and those who wanted to expand it worldwide. The schism grew and Naser said he knew he made the right choice by returning home. Since then, the Jordanian authorities have kept an eye on him; they question him regularly and he has been imprisoned or detained on several occasions, including on suspicion of spreading extremist beliefs.

Naser often mentions that with age he has become less hardened and has less energy, but said he understands the anger and the reasons behind the rise of violence in the region. 'Sunni Muslims in the world are being persecuted and targeted,' he explained. 'Look at the Shia militia groups in Iraq, Iran's support for the government of Syria, and the persecution of Muslims in Burma.'

'Do you consider yourself today a traditional Salafi or a Salafi-Jihadi?' I asked.

'I'm in between now, one day I'm this, one day I'm that. It fluctuates and I keep examining myself, but really I'm in between now,' he said.

'What about when you were younger?'

'I was definitely a Salafi-Jihadi. Everything was either black or white,' he answered.

'So, do you think Fayez is a younger version of yourself back then?'

He replied:

Oh yes, no doubt. For him everything is black or white. Nothing in between. With him it's a one-way path. I tell him, son, life demands some compromise, you must give and take, you must work with the reality on the ground. But to no avail, that's why I worry about him all the time. He's very strict. He told me, 'I'm not going to university,' for example, 'because there are males and females attending the same classes,' so he just won't go. You see my other son, Mustafa, like all my children, I raised him to be a strict believer but like me, he's more diplomatic, he has a way with people. He goes to university; he compromises. But with Fayez I cannot get through to him although he respects me a great deal and just wants to please me. The truth is Fayez is the most sensitive out of all my sons. I saw him watching the news and crying at the massacres being committed against the Syrian people.

In face-to-face interviews with 3,500 young people aged eighteen to twenty-four in sixteen countries, 77 per cent of participants surveyed by the Asda'a Burson-Marsteller Arab Youth Survey said they were concerned about the rise of ISIS, but 76 per cent believed the group would fail in its ultimate goal of establishing a so-called caliphate or state. Although lack of jobs and opportunities was seen by the survey's participants as the main motivating factor for signing up to ISIS, the 2,000 Jordanians who crossed into Syria to join militant groups come from diverse socioeconomic backgrounds, according to Mohammad Abu Rumman. As Naser mentioned, they claimed that they joined the war in Syria to protect the Sunni population there. Some of those militants who returned, including those I saw on trial at the State Security Court, expressed disillusionment with the infighting among various groups within Al-Nusra Front, but also within ISIS.

I also noticed that several of those who returned came from Naser's hometown of Russeifeh. Similarly to the adjacent city of Zarqa, the city is rife with poverty and unemployment; the majority of the city's population is also under twenty-five years old. Naser had lived in Russeifeh nearly all his life. His parents came to Jordan from Palestine in 1962 and settled in Jabal Al-Hussein refugee camp, one of four camps established in Jordan for Palestinian refugees following the 1948 Arab-Israeli war.

The first time I met Naser's mother, Latifa, she knocked lightly at the door of their house to ask if Naser was in. She greeted me with a warm embrace and a kiss on the cheek, taking off her hijab and sitting down to eat. Latifa had given birth to her third son, Naser, when she was nineteen. One of her sons, Omar, had died in the refugee camp when he was only eight months old. Shortly after giving birth to Naser, she had fled the camp because of the poor medical care.

They had moved to Russeifeh, where most of the family still lives. She remembers how forty years ago the area had orchards and fields, cows and apricots, pomegranates and peach trees. Carrots covered vast areas. 'Now we are living in a matchbox,' said Naser. 'It's overcrowded, the city lacks open spaces, green parks, even basic services.' When Naser was a child, his father had searched for better work opportunities and decided to leave his family and move to Germany. He had visited his family once every two or three years but later fell ill, eventually going blind, so he returned home. 'My mother, God bless her, like any other Palestinian woman, became solely responsible for her children,' said Naser.

Illiterate and young, Latifa worked as a farmer, picking parsley, lettuce, rocket, and radishes. Naser told me:

> Even when we had a cow farm, it was my mother who used to do all the work there. She would carry water containers on her head. She would feed the cows and clean after them. She was like a father, a mother, and a brother to me. Not only did my mother go through a hard time on her own, my father, whom I will always love, was a harsh man, so to be honest I wouldn't treat my wife the way my father treated my mother even for a single day.

Naser spent most of his childhood helping his mother in the fields after school. Poverty dominated his formative years. 'I didn't think of the future. When you're living in a rut like that, you're thinking about how to make ends meet, how you're going to get through the next day, not what you can become in twenty years. We didn't have time to dream of the future.'

Looking back on his boyhood, Naser also remembers sharing his daily meals with a cat he owned for seventeen years. He found the cat, Boosey, on the street and bought her a blue collar. When she gave birth to kittens, he recalled, 'I was right there beside her. I emptied a cabinet, lay cloths for her and made sure she was warm.' As was Naser's habit during our conversations, he spoke about the incident and then interjected with a *hadith*, or a report of the words, habits or actions of the Prophet Muhammad. On this occasion, he asked if I knew why Abu Hurayra, a companion of the Prophet who was famous for narrating Muhammad's sayings, was given that name. I shook my head. It would have to have something to do with a cat, because in Arabic *hurayra* means 'little cat', or kitten. Naser told me the story, starting with the death of Abu Hurayra's father, which had left his son to be raised by his mother and no other relatives. Abu Hurayra's name at birth was Abd Al-Shams, or 'Servant of the Sun'. However, as a child, he was often seen playing with a cat and so soon became known as Abu Hurayra, meaning 'Father of the Kitten'.

During his teenage years, Naser remembered that life could have gone one of two ways—it was a choice between drugs and alcohol, or dedicating his life to his religion. 'I chose the latter, and I was willing to let go of my friends if they didn't choose the same path. When I chose this path I can say there was only light and the darkness left me.' Naser is also part of an apolitical movement called Da'wa and Tabligh, whose name means invitation and spreading faith. It urges fellow Muslims to mimic the practices of the Prophet Muhammad in all aspects of life, in rituals, dress, and social behaviour. Like Naser, the group advocates segregation of men and women in public life and that women wear the full-face veil. Critics see the views of people like Naser, who perceive that society has witnessed a deterioration of moral values and deviated from the 'true' Islam, as ultraconservative, and find Salafi practices to be extreme.

When Naser returned from Afghanistan, his father declared it to be high time his son got married and that he would help him find a suitable bride. Naser already had someone in mind, even though he had only caught a glimpse of her three times in his life. 'When I was in Afghanistan, I thought about this lady, my cousin, a lot and I knew she was the person whom I wanted to spend the rest of my life with.' He told his mother and the family proceeded, as is tradition, to ask for her hand in marriage.

When I asked Sarab what her initial impressions of Naser had been, she glanced down shyly at the living room table. They had met in person to have conversation only twice before getting married. Both, however, clearly remember Naser telling his future wife that they would devote their lives to religion and enter heaven together.

I love my wife very much. Some people ask me why I don't have more wives but I'm not interested in marrying anyone else. Not that I am against polygamy, but this is how I personally feel about my situation. We love each other a lot. She is a great woman and she has supported me. When we got married, I told her we would stand together like pillars, side by side, and support each other. It's been more than twenty years and that's how we've been to this day. I have five boys and three girls.

If there is one thing all Naser's neighbours, friends, and family members know about him, it is that Maria, his oldest daughter, is his favourite child; even his seven other children know it. He sometimes teared up when he spoke of her during our conversations. He often speaks of her as a child: the places he used to take her, the anguish of not seeing her when he was in prison, her life now as a mother and more recently as a widow.

Maria was married off when she was just fifteen years old and now has four children, including twins. According to Naser's family, her husband, a Jordanian who initially crossed into Syria to join the Al-Nusra Front and later switched allegiance to ISIS, blew himself up at a military base in northern Iraq on 3 January 2016. I went home and searched the news for details of such an attack. Sure enough, I found a story published by Reuters on that day:

Attacks by five suicide bombers on an Iraqi military base north of Baghdad on Sunday killed at least 15 members of the security forces and wounded 22 others, security sources said. Two of the bombers detonated their vehicle-borne explosives at the western gate of Camp Speicher, a former U.S. base outside the Sunni city of Tikrit. Three others exploded themselves after entering the section of the base where Iraqi police are being trained, police and military sources in the Salahuddin operations command said. Islamic State, the militant group controlling swathes of Iraq's north and west, claimed responsibility for the blasts in a statement distributed by supporters online.

JIHAD IN THE FAMILY: NASER FARHAN

The suicide bomber left a neat handwritten note in red ink for Maria, which she received electronically in March 2016. I read it on Sarab's phone. The letter, captured in a photo, mentions his love for his parents and siblings, naming each of them individually. Then he professes his love for Maria and urges her to take care of their children: no television, no music. Music and some forms of art, including films, are considered corruptive influences by some strict Islamic clerics. He assured her that they would meet in heaven once again.

On that same mobile, I saw photos of a transformed Jordanian man. The first photo is of a young father wearing a white, striped tracksuit. He is standing close to Maria and they are both watching their children play in the snow. He is smiling. I swiped to the right and saw his face in profile, bearded, with a more serious expression. Then another photo of him wearing a traditional brown Arabic cloak with gold trim and a white headscarf or *kufiya*. I swiped again and saw him wearing a longer beard with black cotton pants and a black shirt. He was carrying a weapon.

When Naser first told me the news, I felt compelled to hide my shock and instead asked him how he felt about it. 'It was his fate,' he answered. 'Maria will survive, he was missing for over a year and she had to deal with life on her own in his absence. They told her, he never married another woman when he was away from home. Life without him for Maria will not be easy but this was his fate.' I swiped between the different photos, staring at each one.

I heard a lot about Maria but did not meet her until nearly a year and a half after I met Naser. For months after receiving news of the death of her husband, she refused to leave the house and her mother admitted she was not well. When I met her, she looked pale, her eyes red and puffy, and she barely spoke. Her three sons dashed in and out of Naser's office as Naser cradled her two-year-old daughter in his lap.

Naser doesn't have a strict daily routine. After waking up his younger sons to go to school, he goes to appointments, if there are any, or receives guests in his small porch office. For a while, he was busy regularly attending Fayez's court cases and meeting with a lawyer. He would sometimes drive to visit his brother, Mustafa, who was also in prison. Mustafa had been charged with attempting to cross the border into Syria. 'He went to meet his brother-in-law's wife and children,' Naser explained. 'They were supposed to meet at the border because her husband was killed in Syria, but Mustafa was captured before he reached them.'

Naser was always welcoming and although he did not accept my way of life—my hair is uncovered, and I am a Christian—he was still comfortable sharing his beliefs, thoughts, and even what he called his 'painful childhood memories'. He was also charismatic. In his neighbourhood, he is known as the 'sheikh', or the religious and respected elder who solves marital problems and financial disputes and heals other people's pain with natural herbs and ointments. He was the one who provided for his grandchildren despite his meagre income. When I asked neighbours and people in Russeifeh about him, they expressed their high regard for him but were also aware that he was strict in his beliefs. They spoke of him as a kind person and told me that they turned to him for advice in a neighbourhood that lacked community leaders.

Naser never held a job in either the private or the public sector. He is afraid Fayez will face the same prospects. The only member in the family with a stable job is Abdul Rahman, his oldest son. Naser lives on hope. He has faith in his negotiating skills and status in the community and hopes to receive shares from financial settlements that he mediates, and from his therapy and healing practice. 'Reconciliation is greatly rewarded by God. It's in my nature. I may not make a lot of money but thankfully, I have gained the people's love and trust, which I care about deeply.'

One day, Naser's neighbours begged him to come and see their son, who was a drug addict and was lashing out against his family.

JIHAD IN THE FAMILY: NASER FARHAN

A brief published by CARE, an international humanitarian agency that also operates in Jordan, confirmed something that Naser and his neighbours told me: Russeifeh was suffering from a high rate of school dropouts, family violence, and drug abuse. 'This place is deprived of services, it's more extreme here than other parts of the country and the youth are unemployed. They're frustrated, but when you look around the region, at our neighbours, we are managing.'

Naser took his fourteen-year-old daughter, Razan, out of school a few years ago. 'The school here has a bad environment and even though the girls are separated from the boys, they pass each other since they use the same building but at different times.' Razan resembled her brother Fayez with her gentle features and long flowing brown hair, and always wanted to share baking and beauty tips with me. She confessed she had never liked school or her teachers but still wanted to learn a new craft. Naser's other two daughters also stopped attending school at the same age as Razan.

When I asked Naser if he disagreed with any of the practices implemented by ISIS, like the gruesome beheadings, he would find justifications for them by referring to passages and anecdotes in the Quran or *hadith*. 'I believe in justice, in an eye for an eye, in the implementation of Sharia law.' He sat back on the sofa in his small office, as if reflecting. 'You know, I don't want anything to happen in Jordan, look around you, look at the region. Chaos would erupt and where would we go? There's no place to go. What would I do with my children?'

Naser insisted that his wife cook *maftool*—wheat grains with chicken, chickpeas, and tomato sauce on the side—for me the following week. The day before our meeting, I sent him a message to confirm that we were on. He replied that he might have an event to attend in the evening but that he would let me know soon. I suggested that we meet over tea later in the week instead.

An hour later, he called me to apologize. Sarab had reminded him that I had been invited for lunch and that she had spent the day preparing the meal. 'I will cancel everything if I have to,' he said. 'We are waiting for you.'

When I arrived the next day, his son Mustafa greeted me at the door. Mustafa was the only one in his family to attend university, and was studying engineering. Like his father, he was friendly and welcoming. Naser was in his office with a woman suffering from knee and lower back pain. He had a natural ointment wrapped in a plastic bag, and was reciting verses from the Quran on the topic of healing. The woman wore a black hijab with full make-up. She thanked him as she left. 'I don't ask for money, if people I try to heal give me money I take it, if they don't, I don't,' Naser said, as his two mobile phones rang in the background. Mustafa brought water and spread a large red plastic sheet over the wooden table in the office. Little by little, the food began to appear: sliced green peppers, a tray of *maftool* with barbecued chicken, and a bowl of warm tomato sauce.

Naser liked to eat directly from the tray instead of a plate. He would find a corner and begin to eat around it, adding pieces of chicken and scoops of sauce. I ate from the tray as well, taking the other side. He kept pouring more sauce on my section, if he noticed there was none left. As we ate, he spoke about the wedding of his oldest son, Abdul Rahman. He added that he still had not found an apartment for his son to rent, or at least not one that was affordable. He explained that as a driver (and later an employee at a meat factory), Abdul Rahman would not even be able to cover the apartment's rent with his salary, let alone pay for car fuel, food, clothes, electricity and phone bills.

Meanwhile, Mustafa sat on the other end of the sofa, watching YouTube videos on his phone and half listening to our conversation. He would chime in if he heard us speaking about him, but that day he was mainly preoccupied by his fascination with Japan. 'I hear so many good things about that place and the culture,' Mustafa told me. 'It's my wish to visit it, to see the technology and the future.' Talking about Japan in that small office in the confines of Russeifeh seemed surreal. Japan never seemed so distant to me as it did that afternoon.

When I visited the family again in May 2016 they were discussing and preparing for Fayez's release the following month. Despite their relief, they were worried about him finding work and adjusting to life back at home. Naser told me he hoped the prison sentence would teach him lifelong lessons. Fayez had completed his two-year prison sentence; for part of it he was kept in solitary confinement. When I met with Naser and his family in July 2016, they introduced me to Fayez. He had shoulder-length black, wavy hair and a beard, and was one month shy of his twentieth birthday.

In the beginning, he would only answer my questions with 'yes' or 'no'. I asked him how he had spent his days in prison, what he did all day. 'I only thought about the actual day I was going to be released. When you're in there, you only think how you're going to get out of this place, you play volleyball with the other young men, you read the Quran, you pray, that's all.'

Fayez was in twelfth grade when he was detained, so had not graduated or even completed the mandatory high school exam. When I mentioned education, he seemed reluctant to return to school. 'I really don't know what I'll do with my life now,' Fayez said:

> I think I just need to get used to the idea that I'm not in prison anymore. It takes time and I know I'm being watched, but I'm also free. I'm trying to remind myself I'm free. The security services told me, 'We know your every move, we know who you talk to, who comes to visit you.' I know that but inside me, I always have my faith. It's what saved me while in prison. It's what is always inside me.

Naser stood up and excused himself. It was prayer time. On his feet were the black slippers that he wore all the time, except in winter. As he leaned against the door, Fayez stood up and looked at his father. 'Wait for me,' he said. 'I'm coming with you. I'm right behind you.'

4

SURVIVOR IN EXILE

AMAL SAWAAN

Her grim, crooked, half-finished home had been built in haste, bound to leak. No one seemed comfortable in that home, except for two rats who hid in the pipes and could occasionally be heard making scraping sounds. Out of desperation, Amal Sawaan, a refugee who had fled to Jordan with her family to escape the civil war in Syria, had rented the house before it had been completed: no roof, no door, no privacy.

Amal contemplates getting rid of the rats, but, like her, their fate remains in limbo. For now, she has trapped them by placing heavy white stones on top of the only two holes they can escape from.

We met at her home for the first time on a cold and cloudy December afternoon in 2016. The family of four—Amal, her husband and their two teenage boys—congregated around one small propane gasoline heater to stay warm. The same heater is used to boil tea and coffee, and sometimes serves as a stove for cooking meals.

Amal is thirty-nine years old and divides her life into three distinct parts: before the war, during the war, and as a refugee in Jordan.

'Three years and nine months,' Amal answered quickly, when I asked her how long she had been in Jordan. She spoke softly at first. Her answers were brief and barely audible. 'I can't say life is difficult here but I can't say it's easy either,' she sighed. 'Even if it were easy, there's nothing like one's own country, one's own home.'

When the civil war began, many of the Syrians pouring over the border that I spoke to, like Iraqis and Palestinians before them, told me that they would be returning home as soon as the war ended. They waited, as their lives came to a juddering halt. But days turned to months, and then to years. As this brutal conflict enters its eighth year, thoughts of returning have evaporated for most. Navigating a dizzying humanitarian aid system, they sign up with the United Nations to officially be recognized as refugees instead. Some refugees register their children in schools, while adults continually learn new crafts and skills just to survive. Others are forced to work, sometimes illegally.

Chaotic and crime-ridden refugee camps have become idle and systematized, demonstrating the state of ambivalence and uncertainty that is becoming increasingly common with refugee displacements across the Middle East. Host countries prepare for short-term stays that end up stretching into years. 'I was impressed at the detailed planning that appears to have gone into Azraq [refugee camp],' wrote Fabian Hamilton, UK parliamentarian and shadow minister for peace and disarmament, in an email to me when he visited Jordan in 2017 on an official mission. 'The array of solar panels which ultimately aim to make the camp energy-independent; the bore holes which are tapping into water aquifers 500 metres below the surface to reduce dependence on water tankers delivering to the camp ...'

Months may have become years, but Amal has never forgotten her home. She was born and raised in Homs, the third largest city in Syria after Aleppo and Damascus. 'I still think about my house in Syria.' Amal, whose name means 'hope' in Arabic, slowly stirred a pot of thick black coffee on top of the propane heater and wistfully added, 'I think about the life I had there.'

Once a diverse and industrial town, Homs became a stronghold for opposition groups against the Syrian government, which launched a massive assault on the city in May 2011. Prior to the war, this key agricultural town produced corn, wheat, cotton, fruit and vegetables and was home to Christians, Sunnis, and Alawites who all lived and worked together. Amal and her family lived through the bombardment and siege that left most of the city destroyed and thousands of its residents dead. In 2015, the government claimed victory after ousting the last remaining rebels, who evacuated the city.

As a child, Amal spent most of her time at her grandparents' home, also in Homs, where she had received the attention she yearned for as the oldest of ten siblings. She had attended a public school for girls, where she had many friends and loved Arabic language class. She would spend her afternoons crocheting and had wanted to become a teacher.

> I grew up in the middle of the city, mainly at my grandparents' traditionally styled Syrian home, which had a central courtyard shielding the family's privacy and large rooms surrounding it. It had a garden and a water fountain in the corner. My grandparents practically raised me and if you asked me what life was like, I would say it was wonderful.

In ninth grade, Amal fell in love. She met her future husband, a relative, at her grandparents' home. Farhan, who was six years older than Amal, didn't want her to continue with her education, so at the age of fourteen she dropped out of school. She still spent most of her days at her grandparents' house and kept in touch with school friends. To the dismay of both of their families, Amal and Farhan met there regularly and five years later, they got married.

> No one approved of our relationship. It was my own decision. I remained strong and I had to bear everything on my own because it was my choice. My parents disapproved of him because he came from a lower social class. His parents disapproved of me and wanted him to marry someone else. Just because we were in love, they hated me right away.

The first house Amal and Farhan moved into in Al-Sabeel district in Homs was not unlike the home they settled into as refugees in Jordan. It was empty and cold with no heating, not even a propane gas heater. There were no mattresses or any other furniture. When Farhan was still single, he worked at his family's bakery in Homs, but he was fired after he decided to marry Amal. He took any odd job he could find and Amal sold her jewellery to manage daily expenses. In 2000, Amal became pregnant with her first son, Hamza, and had to borrow money from a friend and an aunt to cover medical expenses, including an emergency caesarean delivery.

After she was released from hospital, it was crucial for Amal to work if she wanted to survive. She started crocheting again and embroidered entire dresses, at first to sell to shop owners, but before long to sell directly to neighbours and friends. Amal's income paid the rent. 'My husband worked as a driver for a distribution company but it wasn't stable work, so I had to support him because no one else was.' She opened the cigarette pack lying next to her empty coffee cup and lit a cigarette. She gazed at the ring of fire from the propane gas and reflected, 'It was then that I regretted not continuing with my education.'

At that moment, Amal and Farhan's eldest son, Hamza, walked into the house. He was tall and lanky, with a shy smile. After school, he worked at a clothing store folding shirts and selling them to help support his family. According to a 2016 survey by the International Labour Organization (ILO), the number of child labourers in Jordan had doubled to nearly

70,000 since 2007 despite efforts to crack down on street ped-
dlers and to enforce workplace regulations.

The survey also revealed that Syrians have the lowest school
attendance rate in Jordan compared to Jordanians and other
groups, but also the lowest wages when working, exposing them
to a greater risk of exploitation. Many Syrian families send their
children to work out of desperation, but also for fear that if the
father or the adult in the family were caught working illegally,
they would be deported back to Syria. At fourteen years old,
Hamza risked being detained by police for working underage, but
often Syrian refugee children would be released shortly after
being taken to the police station.

Over 10 million Syrians have been displaced from their homes
since the civil war began in March 2011, of whom more than
650,000 have registered with the UN Refugee Agency in Jordan.
Amal and her family live in the northern town of Mafraq, close
to the Syrian border and home to nearly 80,000 Syrians who fled
the war. The town's population has more than doubled with the
new influx, straining the public school system and scarce water
resources, further shelving any plans that aimed at ending the
double shift school system. Typically, Jordanian children attend
school in the morning, and Syrians in the afternoon. In 2013,
when I visited Mafraq to interview refugees, bin lorries were
unable to keep up with the load, and rubbish was left burning
inside metal tips, turning them charcoal black.

Amal's current home has two rooms, with a blanket serving as
a curtain to separate the living room from the small kitchen area
she had cobbled together. Behind the curtain lay one of the white
square tiles to prevent the rats from escaping. Her living room had
several thin, beige, floral-designed mattresses and a small television. Between the television and propane heater, a window overlooked the cement wall of their neighbours' house—a Jordanian
family. The two homes were separated by a garbage-strewn alley-

way—empty yoghurt cartons and crushed Pepsi cans, a reminder of how stretched the town's infrastructure had become.

A ten-minute drive east of Mafraq takes you to the Zaatari refugee camp, the second largest refugee camp in the world, housing almost 80,000 Syrians and a lively market built by and for the refugees. Amal and her family had spent three days in the camp when they first arrived in Jordan. They recall being exhausted, fearful, and shocked from what they had seen and left behind.

The conflict in Syria, part of a wider wave of 2011 Arab Spring protests, grew out of discontent with Syrian President Bashar Al-Assad's government. It quickly escalated into an armed conflict after protests calling for his removal were violently suppressed. Before the war came to Homs, life for Amal had been moving forward. Demand for her handiwork had flourished, her husband had a steadier job, and they had moved to an apartment she loved and had hoped to own someday. She developed close friendships with her neighbours, both of her sons were attending school, and the family spent weekends in a popular forest area called Al-Waer, west of Homs hugging the Orontes river, which weaves its way through the city all the way from the Bekaa Valley in the west to Antioch in the north. Amal would bake desserts, pack tea bags, and bring coffee in thermos mugs to keep it warm.

The family would go to the forest every Friday evening and return home at two in the morning. They would spend the evening barbecuing meat and chicken. At a nearby playground, both parents kicked a ball around with their two boys and taught them how to ride a bike. Amal suddenly paused in the middle of recounting these family excursions, and then began to cry.

Today the area of Al-Waer in Homs is synonymous with abandonment and evacuation, after years of military siege and bombardment. In March 2017, several buses drove out of the Al-Waer district and thousands of rebels and civilians evacuated in batches under a Russian-backed deal with the Assad regime. The Syrian

Observatory for Human Rights, a British-based monitoring group, said the buses had mainly headed north to Aleppo and that when the operation was complete, it 'marked the biggest evacuation during the war out of one Syrian district, home to about 40,000 civilians and more than 25,000 rebels.'

Right before the war, people began to envy our life, really. Everything in our life was changing for the better. When there is understanding between a loving couple, nothing else really matters. Money came and went. In my new apartment, there was warmth and tenderness. It was an apartment with a living room, bigger than this one. It had several rooms, including a guest room, living room, a bedroom for the boys, and our bedroom. It had an entrance outside, and it was a first-story apartment. There was a patio with white chairs and a matching table. It was filled with plants, white devil's ivy with green leaves. It was as if the ivy climbed the walls. We used to say, 'Well that's one crazy plant.' We had shiny lemon leaves, and Arabian jasmine. My house was lovely. It was nicely furnished. It was a lovely life. Every morning, my neighbours and I would visit each other and have coffee. I would have a cigarette with the coffee as well—some of the neighbours joined in but others wouldn't go near a cigarette. My main concern was to buy the house. I paid the owner half its price. I also thought, 'Perhaps now that I am more settled, I will have a daughter.' Then the war happened and everything was lost, just like it was for everyone else. My building was destroyed. As for my neighbours, some of them died; some are in Syria; others are in Germany and France.

On Friday, 15 March 2011, the protests began in Amal's neighbourhood. The weekend trips to the forest stopped. Residents went food shopping on Thursdays, knowing that the following day there would be demonstrations. For a while, Amal could not see the clashes and only heard the protestors' chants from a distance.

Slowly, the signs of impending war started to appear: checkpoints, young men carrying guns, deteriorating medical services.

'The voices became louder and trouble, we thought, was closer than ever.' Amal began fearing for her husband when he went to make deliveries and insisted on accompanying him. He drove to cities and remote villages that became sites of clashes between the regime and the rebels.

Then the war knocked on Amal's door. Her youngest son Mohammad was hit in the eye by a small piece of bullet shrapnel while he stood on his neighbour's apartment balcony. Amal's mother-in-law, who lived nearby, took her grandson to the doctor but the family was advised to send him to a specialist. Amal called an optometrist who saw Mohammad earlier.

> Before I could continue, he said, 'Oh isn't he the one who can't see anymore in one eye?' When he said that, I fell to the ground. I fainted. I said, 'What do you mean he can't see?' The doctor was examining Mohammad and told me not to worry, that he had retinal detachment from the injury and had to undergo an operation. 'We'll remove the fluid behind the retina and he will be okay,' he said. You know, my son was six years old at the time, but I was shocked because he didn't express any pain. Then I began to sell everything I had, so we could pay for the operation.

The operation did not go as planned. Mohammad woke up during the procedure, and had to be given a second dose of anaesthesia. When the doctors had completed the operation, Mohammad's 'colour was all white,' his mother recalled, 'as if all the blood in his body was sucked out of him.' Meanwhile, there were clashes outside the clinic. Hospitals had routinely become a target in the Syrian conflict. According to the medical humanitarian agency Doctors Without Borders, access to medical care in many parts of Syria is dire. Many hospitals are routinely in short supply as health workers have fled or been killed.

Amal took Mohammad and went home. There were snipers on the rooftops, gunfire in the streets, loud noises. Some roads were blocked, forcing Amal to re-route. When she arrived with her son, Farhan carried him and lay him on his bed. He then told Amal he had to leave for work.

> I told Farhan, 'Don't go to work.' It was the first time I had ever told him not to go. He told me there was no one else to make the delivery. I took his hand and kissed it. It was the first time I had ever done that. I said, 'For God's sake, don't go. Please, don't go. Just today, don't go.' He told me not to worry, that this was work and he had to do it. He asked me why I was worried. I told him not to leave Mohammad and me on our own. He left. As soon as he left our neighbourhood, I heard loud voices in the street, saying, 'The neighbourhood is surrounded by soldiers, the neighbourhood is under siege. There is a raid.' I opened the window and asked our neighbour—no, I remember I yelled, 'What's going on?' She told me the neighbourhood was sealed from all sides. There was no way in or out.

Amal paused and again started to cry as she remembered that day. Mohammad, she said, had still been unconscious with a fever. 'He was limp as a cloth, as if he were dead, God forbid.' The electricity went out in the neighbourhood. Amal's neighbours didn't leave her side. Still, she said, she had felt helpless. No one she knew slept that night. The next morning, she went to the military checkpoint despite her neighbours' pleas to her not to do so. It was crucial, she told them, to leave and seek medical help. It was a matter of life and death for her son.

Meanwhile, Farhan was unable to return home; he was essentially locked out. When Amal approached the checkpoint for the first time, she left Mohammad with her neighbours. The streets she once knew so well seemed suddenly foreign to her, filled with young men and guns. 'It was a street war,' she said. 'We didn't know what was going on.'

When Amal went to Farhan's family and asked them to walk with her to the checkpoint to seek help for her son, they told her they were too afraid to leave their home. She went instead with an elderly woman who lived down the road from her family. She told the military officer at the checkpoint that her son was ill so she needed to leave the neighbourhood to get help. The officer looked at her, she recalled, and said he would let her out only if she brought back one of the young men standing in the distance. 'They wanted to capture, detain, recruit, torture, kill. I didn't know what they would do to any of them.' She asked the officer if there was any other way out. 'No, he said, bring one of those young men with you and I'll let you out.'

She returned home disappointed. An elderly man, also named Farhan, heard her story and volunteered to carry her son and accompany her to the checkpoint. When she agreed, they walked to the checkpoint and the same officer chided her for bringing an older man with her. Then he received a call from a soldier, telling him that they had occupied a building nearby. The caller told the officer to confiscate all three identification cards and to let them pass, but Amal explained that without her ID, she would not be able to pass through other checkpoints. The officer agreed to write down their names instead and told her that they had two hours to return to the neighbourhood.

Amal finally arrived at a clinic full of patients. Farhan, the older man who accompanied her, was losing patience. He repeatedly told the doctors that they had only two hours before they both had to return home. He told them, Amal recalled, that he had left his wife and children behind in their neighbourhood to help Amal and her son. No one seemed to listen to him. 'He then punched the glass window, shattering it, just so the doctor would come out and let us in. And they let us in despite the loud protestations from other patients.'

Mohammad eventually regained consciousness and was given medication. Farhan, the man who was with Amal, took her to his relatives nearby, so her husband could meet her there and give her some bread, money, and medication for Mohammad before she returned home. On their way back, she received a call from her neighbours, who urged her to get back quickly, informing her that their neighbourhood was 'being ruined' by heavy fighting. Amal could hear the gunfire in the background and insisted she return with the old man, whom she described as sacrificing his life for her son.

Amal got back to her neighbourhood amidst a barrage of gunfire. Soldiers there told Amal and Farhan to hurry back to their homes. The two went their separate ways and Amal found her neighbours waiting for her at the entrance of their building. They took Mohammad from her and she washed her face, had a drink of water, and finally sat down. Two hours later, the gunfire subsided and the neighbourhood was calm. People began going out in the streets again. The army withdrew from the neighbourhood by sunset. Then, Amal recalled, one of her neighbours called her name.

'Um Hamza [mother of Hamza]! Amal!' he was yelling. My neighbour was panicking. I opened the door and asked, 'What is it?' He panted, 'Farhan, the man who went with you and Mohammad today, is gone. He is dead.' They had destroyed his house with a tank. Just because he went out with me. Just because they saw him at the checkpoint. They took his name, and anyone who had a personal grudge could do whatever they wanted. It was chaos. There was revenge. Just like what happened in Iraq. That night, Iraq happened. Farhan, my husband, came back. I was so upset with him. I didn't want to talk to him because he had left me despite my pleas for him not to do so. He told me, 'Amal, you know what happened to me? I reached the neighbourhood and found that it was under siege and there was no way to enter. I took another road and got arrested and beaten up.' To this day, his back still hurts him from the beating. They arrested him and beat him up on the street. They hit him with the shotgun like this. He said there was a passenger with him with no ID, so they took them both out of the car and beat them up. I knew then and there that the war was becoming more dangerous.

Day by day, things got worse for Amal and her family. Food was becoming more scarce and the shooting took on an increasingly random pattern. Once a stray bullet went through Amal's kitchen window. She was standing by the kitchen sink, but miraculously was not injured. Soon a tank entered the neighbourhood. Whenever it fired, the walls of the house would shake.

One October day in 2011, Amal went out with her neighbour to buy food. They agreed to stop at a clothing shop on the main road nearby, where Amal wanted to buy her two children new clothes for the upcoming Muslim festival of Eid. Amal's neighbour brought her son with her, and Amal brought twelve-year-old Hamza, leaving Mohammad at home with another neighbour.

They were about to enter the shop when they heard gunshots. A tank began firing in the street. It was a cold day, Amal recalled, and when the tank began firing, she had felt death coming closer.

There was nothing left but death. The tank was shooting and there was glass everywhere. We fell to the ground. There was blood on the floor inside. All I was thinking of was how to protect Hamza. I looked up and saw a column in a corner. I thought that the bullets wouldn't be able to go through the column, so I hid Hamza behind it. This went on for fifteen minutes or a little longer. The bullets would come and go and the glass would shatter. The glass broke and the shop was ruined, with us trapped inside. I had Hamza safe behind the column. The shop owner was with us. I told my neighbour, 'Let's try and get out of here.' There were two other women in the store as well. We planned to escape as soon as the tank moved away. When it did, some of us left and some of us stayed. Then it came back and we couldn't move. Then it went away again and we escaped. Thank God, we all made it out safely.

It was raining outside. The streets were full of men taking part in the street war. I didn't know them. I don't even remember their faces. One of them told me, 'Don't be scared.' I was scared, crying, hugging

Hamza, and running. There were gunshots right behind us. It was just like what you see on television. I was running. He said, 'Don't be scared, you're safe now.' I said, 'What safety are you talking about? You are the ones making them shoot at us. Why are you doing this? Who's going to pay the price? The price is our safety and the destruction of our homes.' I said this to the young men carrying guns. I began yelling at them and cursing them. 'When you want to shoot, go over there to the other side. Don't attack them from amongst our homes and alleys.' I was yelling and it was cold. They started telling me stuff about religion and I don't know what. I asked, 'What religion are you talking about? What God are you talking about? Do you know God?'

It took Amal and Hamza two hours to reach the diminishing safety of their home. In the end, her brother told her to leave their neighbourhood and to come to his. He lived in an area called Siteen Street, nearly half an hour's drive from Amal's neighbourhood. At the beginning of the war, Amal and her neighbours had made a pact: they would stay, no matter how violent the war became.

I didn't want to leave my house. My neighbours and I didn't want to leave. I mean, where were we going to go? My entire life was here. I didn't want to go anywhere else. Farhan would say to me each week, 'For God's sake, let us leave. Let us go to your parents. Let us go to your brother. Let's go anywhere. Let's just go for a while, then come back.' I always said no. I didn't want to go. He said our apartment building was beginning to collapse on us. I kept on refusing. He said, 'You can't even go get food for the house anymore. Every time you go out there, there is shooting.'

Amal finally gave in. They left the house carrying only their ID cards and two brightly coloured tracksuits, one for each son. It would be the last time the family saw their home. Three days later, while they were at her brother's house, people from Amal's neighbourhood called and told her that her house was in ruins, destroyed. They said that she wouldn't be able to return and that the last remaining people in the neighbourhood were escaping.

> Nothing that could happen after that mattered to me. My life's dream, my kingdom, was gone. And that's the story of all of Syria, unfortunately. I sometimes console myself by saying this didn't happen to me alone. I collapsed. I stopped eating. I stopped drinking. I was lost now.

By winter 2012, nearly a year after the civil war began in Syria, Amal realized she had to remain strong because, she noted, her two children and her husband depended on her. Not wanting to feel like she and her family were a burden, she moved from her brother's apartment to her aunt's apartment building in Al-Asheereh, a neighbourhood only ten minutes away by car. Her aunt's family moved to the ground floor and Amal and her family occupied an apartment they had once rented out on the top floor. Amal and her family borrowed clothes from neighbours, friends, and relatives. They laid out mattresses and pillows and stayed there for a month and a half. On Thursday, 8 March 2012, Amal's brother visited their aunt and told them they needed to leave the neighbourhood because of an impending military raid. The government was searching and detaining people who were on a 'wanted list'. Having set up a temporary home, and with the promising prospect of work sewing business suits, Amal was horrified at the thought of being displaced again.

> I said, 'No, don't tell me to leave, I'm not leaving.' My brother said that we would go stay at his friend's house for a week and return. He did everything he could to convince me. I refused. Then I said, 'Okay, let's wait until Friday, we can leave on Friday evening.' The raid was supposed to be on Saturday morning. I told him, 'I have some laundry to do and I need to tidy up some things, then I'll go with you.' I washed the clothes on Thursday evening, bathed the kids and arranged everything. There was a power outage at night. We spent some time with my aunt, then went upstairs to bed.

Farhan told me to blow out the candles and to go to sleep, but we never slept.

Then the sound of gunfire began. She heard the familiar sound of tank shelling. She looked outside the window and saw people running away. Farhan and Amal picked up the children and ran outside. Many families were in the streets, running east, away from the tanks that were approaching from the west. Meanwhile, Amal's family escaped in her brother's car and drove for nearly an hour to a neighbourhood called Awras. Her brother dropped her off at a market called Al-Hasheesh, where her father picked her up.

Amal's family spent their final year in Syria in the village of Mahin on the outskirts of Homs, almost an hour and a half away from the last neighbourhood they had fled. Amal's family and her parents lived together in a spacious unfurnished house. A friend of her father's had managed to convince the owners of the house, who were residing in Kuwait at the time, to let them stay there free of charge. A year later, Farhan insisted they leave Syria altogether, because the future seemed so uncertain; he could no longer find work. Even though there was a semblance of normalcy in their lives with both boys attending school again, he told Amal that war followed them everywhere and it would soon catch up with them. Amal refused to leave at first, but eventually, she relented.

Her brother's friend was waiting for them. He had purchased bus tickets to Al-Nabek on the outskirts of Damascus, paid for by her brother, who had already made the journey to Jordan with his family, and who has since resettled in France. There were dozens of military checkpoints on the way. 'Every time we stopped, we thought either that we would either be sent back, or that we would die,' recalled Amal. Everyone on the bus was questioned and searched by military soldiers. They were asked where they were coming from and where they were going.

They drove for an hour more to a Damascus suburb called Al-Kisweh, around 13 kilometres south of Damascus. They were stopped at a bridge where they had to take another bus heading to Daraa, a city in southwestern Syria, located about 13 kilometres north of the border with Jordan. Many cars approached the buses, and the passengers on board thought that they were people coming to help. They quickly realized that they were *shabiha*, a term to describe armed militiamen in support of the Syrian regime.

> They yelled at us to come down and they placed the men in a line facing a wall; the women stood by the pavement. The people started to descend the steps of the bus, but I began to feel a bit dizzy. I looked behind me and my sister fell on top of me, unconscious. I began to scream, 'She's dead, Farhan!' The *shabiha* asked me, 'Who's Farhan?' They went and brought him to me. At that moment, when they were distracted with my sister, I saw a man we knew run away. They put us back on the bus and took us to another checkpoint. It was then that they took the men and they began to torture them in front of us. They began kicking them and then used a cable to whip them on their backs, including Farhan. I went to help him but they turned me back. They cursed at us, the women, and they took our money, mobile phones and if any of the women had gold, they stole it. At one point, our men were taken into a room and we could no longer see them. The *shabiha* would say, 'Why do you want to go to Jordan? Do you want to be refugees? What will Jordan offer you? You don't like your own country?' The man who ran away must have gone and told people about us, because at sunset, we saw Red Crescent employees pulling up in a car. I saw Farhan and they made us sign papers that we would not attempt to go to Jordan again and the buses dropped us at a mosque called Othman bin Afan in Daraya, a Damascus suburb.

Amal and her family stayed at the mosque for four days. Others who were with them ran away earlier but Farhan was too afraid to leave. After four days, they walked out and kept on walking for an hour until they managed to arrange to meet with the same bus driver who was supposed to have taken them four days earlier to Daraa. The bus driver asked for additional money, but Amal told him they had already paid him and had nearly paid with their lives riding with him. They took the bus on 3 February 2013 to Daraa and that same day crossed into the Jordanian desert through Tal Shehab, a major entry point into Jordan for Syrian refugees.

At the time, all they needed to enter Jordan was their identification cards. They were taken by bus to Zaatari refugee camp in Mafraq. The Jordanian military, however, sealed the country's last entry points for Syrian refugees on 21 June 2016, after a suicide bomber detonated a car bomb near the border, killing four Jordanian soldiers, a police officer, and a civil defence officer.

By the time Amal arrived in Jordan, she had been internally displaced eight times since the war in Syria began, eight times in under two years. She entered the country carrying a small bag with undergarments for both of her sons, her own thin black wristwatch and a worn-out wallet. She was wearing a faded velvet robe with four diamond-shaped buttons and a zip. She still hangs it in her home behind the bedroom door as a reminder of the harrowing journey. In winter, she sometimes wears it.

When they arrived as refugees, they found a stark contrast between Syrian soldiers and the Jordanian soldiers who met them at the border. The Jordanians welcomed them, helped them with their bags. Amal recalled the way they had helped parents carry their babies or any sick children. A soldier gave his mobile phone to Amal so she could call her brother. From the time they were at the mosque until the day she arrived in Jordan, Amal had lost touch with her family, and they did not know her whereabouts, or if she was even still alive.

The soldiers and aid workers helped the refugees board the bus to the camp, where they were provided with blankets and slept in a large tent with others. At the time, the camp was still unorganized, theft was rampant, and there was no electricity. It was initially built in nine days, in a dry dusty desert that is too cold in winter and too hot in summer. The women were too afraid to use the bathrooms, rectangular concrete block structures built far from the tents.

The next day, Amal's brother, Wasel, whom she had not seen for the past year and a half, came to pick her up, and they went to his home in Mafraq.

'When my brother arrived,' Amal told me, 'I felt like I had everything I could ever need. He told me, "Now you'll be able to take a shower, we have new clothes for you and the family. We have cooked you a hot meal. You can eat and rest properly."'

In Jordan, Amal regained a sense of safety. Her two sons began attending school again. Still, on a personal level, new challenges arose. Her husband Farhan began behaving strangely. Amal was left to navigate through streets she did not know and to seek help on her own from aid agencies. Her husband, she said, did nothing all day. She would leave early in the morning searching for an affordable home to rent, to enrol her children in a public school nearby, to find food rations and register her family as refugees, while he did nothing but sleep. When she came back home, she would find him lying on the couch, smoking cigarettes and no longer wanting to talk to his family. 'He became a different person,' Amal remembered. 'He no longer wanted to be involved in our lives.' Farhan became completely dependent on Amal but still wanted to make the decisions at home. She grew resentful and tired. Their relationship went through its worst times after they became refugees.

When she went to aid agencies during the day, she would wait by the entrance and watch Syrians registering and receiving aid. She would stand there on her own and cry.

> I was shocked at the state that people were in, I was shocked to see what happened to the Syrian people. It reached a point where if someone asked me if I was Syrian, I would deny it. I was embarrassed

to admit that I was Syrian because of what I was seeing. What we have come to, begging for food, for aid, for medicine.

The same day she went to the aid agency, she insisted on moving out of her brother's home. She found the home she lives in now. It was winter and the owners asked her if she was sure she wanted to live there even if it was only half finished. She borrowed money from her aunt and paid for the first month. When she moved in that evening, she slept on the floor. 'There was nothing,' she remembered, 'not even a roof, as I mentioned, but at least it was my home for now.'

The rats, too, have been there ever since. Amal collects aid from different agencies, mainly for food rations and a discount on some medicines. A local church nearby provides her with help as well. The church offers English classes for free, and Amal sends her children there. Three times a week, she works for a German non-profit organization, leading best practice sessions on motherhood for other refugee women. Just recently Farhan began working at a shoe shop from morning until evening, but both of their jobs together barely cover the rent.

The last time I visited Amal, I took her out for lunch at a restaurant near her home. The market was bustling with people; neon signs promoting Syrian desserts and Syrian pastries were visible all along the road. She was suffering from advanced hyperthyroidism, which was causing her body pain, sleepless nights, and mood swings. She barely ate her barbecue chicken and picked at a side order of coleslaw. We packed up her plate of chicken and bread and took it back home. When we returned, Amal's son Hamza was lying on his bed reading messages on his phone. He stood up when we entered the room. He was much taller but also much skinnier than when I had last seen him. His mother complained that he refused to continue attending English classes at the church.

As we were seated in the main room, Hamza told his mother that Hanna had arrived outside. Hanna, who volunteers at the church and works with aid agencies, has been in contact with the family for a long time. As the guest sat across the room, he spoke quickly as if in a hurry. 'I'm here and I have some wonderful news,' Hanna told Amal as Hamza looked down at his feet. Through a Canadian church, a family in British Columbia was seeking to sponsor a Syrian refugee family of four, including two children. Although there were four families that matched the criteria, Amal's family was chosen at the end. By May 2017, Hanna said the process might take up to six months.

Amal began to cry. She told him she did not want to leave. She knew everyone else in her family wanted to. She had seen her brother leave Jordan for France. The aunt they stayed with in Homs for one and a half months had resettled in Germany. The rest of her family saw life in Jordan as little more than a temporary measure, but she was beginning, after three years, to feel as if it was becoming more permanent. Hanna told her to think of the future, to think of her children, her ambitions to continue her education and find work, and for Farhan to find a stable job. He told her to consider the kind of healthcare they would receive there. She buried her face in her hands and cried.

Amal's dream is to return to Syria one day. Being in Jordan, close to her country's border, had brought her comfort, no matter how illusory. When we were at the restaurant the last time I saw her, she asked me if I would drive her to the border town nearby, just to catch a glimpse of her war-torn nation. For her, leaving for Canada meant her dream of returning home was being stripped away. When Hanna came with news about Canada, she told him it was a one-way ticket to an unknown place, where her boys would grow up, drift away, and speak a language she did not know. She would have no control over her life again and whatever lay ahead, she was being displaced once again, torn forever from the land that she once called home. 'Syria,' sighed Amal, 'will only be stored memories.'

5

THE DECIDER

JERIES AKROUSH

Jeries is a heavy smoker and a man of few words. Seldom does he smile but when he does, his dark face lights up. He is a civil servant by day and a real estate agent by late afternoon. As a bureaucrat for the past twenty-five years, he finds comfort in routine and familiarity. As a real estate agent, he finds excitement in field work and big deals.

Jeries was born and raised in Fuheis, a traditional town built in the eighteenth century, located northwest of Amman. The town has numerous churches, hundred-year-old stone cottages and a roundabout with a faded bronze-coloured statue of Saint George killing the dragon. Although famous for its farms and scenic views, it's yet another place that has transformed due to urbanization and a growing population. Rows of shops have expanded onto hilltops and slopes. Restaurants, cafés and apartment buildings continue to rise.

In some ways, it is an entirely different place from the one where Jeries grew up. In other ways, it is exactly the same. 'It used to be a village, not a town,' he corrected me. 'The streets weren't even paved when I was growing up here. The main street you see outside, it wasn't even a street back then. It was a dirt road that was 3 metres wide.'

Fuheis' population is predominantly Christian. There are nearly 250,000 Christians in Jordan, but their numbers have been decreasing due to high immigration rates to the West, mainly due to economic opportunities and lower birth rates than in Muslim-majority countries. Although they make up only 3 per cent of the country's population, Jordanian Christians remain an influential community. They are engaged in parliamentary and political affairs, civil service and commerce.

During the Arab Spring, Christians across the Middle East expected new governments to improve human rights but elections in many countries, like Egypt, delivered mandates to Islamist political parties like the Muslim Brotherhood. Meanwhile, civil conflicts like in Syria and the fall of dictators like Libya's Muammar Gaddafi left behind a vacuum that benefitted extremists and criminals. This gave rise to the emergence of the Islamic State, which targeted minorities including Iraqi and Syrian Christians, some of whom fled and continue to reside in Jordan.

Jeries, who is forty-nine years old, attended the Patriarch Latin School, a private institution. He remembers walking to school every day during the 1970s. His four children today attend the same school he did when he was a boy, but he can't imagine them walking there. 'Life was simple back then,' he reflected, blowing a puff of smoke one Saturday morning at his small real estate office.

In many ways, Jeries relishes simplicity and order: the less paperwork, the better. Short responses to extended questions. Arriving at decisions, with little hesitation. And so, it came as no surprise when he noted that his mandatory service in the Jordanian Armed Forces was 'the best thing I did in my life.'

THE DECIDER: JERIES AKROUSH

When he completed high school, he had aspired to become a lawyer and attend university in Egypt.

His plans fell through after his father declared that he could not afford the tuition fees. Since he did not attend college, military service was compulsory for two years. 'It gave me a purpose and a sense of achievement,' recalled Jeries. A ruling was issued in 1976 by royal decree for mandatory military service or 'active duty'. Exemptions were made for those who could not pass a requisite medical examination due to a permanent disability, or those who were the only sons or brothers of men who had died while serving in the armed forces. Jordan cancelled conscription after signing a peace treaty with Israel in 1994.

> The first time I served in the army, I was dispatched to the Jordan Valley. We trained there for months. It was not easy, of course. It was December. It was cold—no, it was freezing, I remember, and we used to sleep in tents. We didn't have showers. I used to go on a hilltop in the cold weather, take a bucket of water and some soap and pour it on myself. The hardships create camaraderie. I would be assigned at 2 a.m. to guard the soldiers sleeping. I wasn't the only one, of course. We were on rotation but when it was my turn, I would look at all the soldiers sleeping and feel a great sense of responsibility. I was guarding them. When we were training, we felt we were doing something great.

The first time I approached Jeries, a manager at the Civil Status and Passport Department, he was standing at the manager's office and holding stacks of paper ready for signing. He glanced quickly at me, as if searching for the precise reason for my visit. Before I had a chance to explain, Jeries dashed quickly into another office, and then returned.

He led me to his desk. Behind him was a window with a view of a historic limestone home, sealed with grass-green-painted steel doors. Next to his desk, there were several employees sitting behind glass partitions with openings only large enough for papers and passports to slip through. Voices of customers were drowned out by the clicking clatter of computer keyboards. Mobile phones beeped, whistled and rang. Next to the computers there were stamps, ashtrays, paper coffee cups, and mostly half empty tea glasses with fresh mint leaves still stubbornly sticking to the round edges.

When I informed Jeries that I hoped to learn more about his life and work, he cut the conversation short. 'That's fine. So, what is required of me?' he asked.

We met a week later at his real estate office, located on a slope and tucked between a pharmacy, a hair salon, and a shop bursting with household items that obstructed the pavement. He met me at the door, cigarette pack in hand. At the entrance is a round table where he meets with clients and receives guests. The other room is an office with a desk and a view from the window of sand patches, grass, olive trees and yellow rocks neatly stacked on top of each other, acting as low walls between a few scattered homes.

Jeries poured me a cup of Arabic coffee, served more often in Jordan at funerals, weddings, or other celebrations as a sign of hospitality. The coffee beans are lightly or heavily brewed and often cardamom is added. Jeries doesn't like cardamom. 'Plain coffee,' he noted. 'Just plain.' He sat back behind his desk.

'Do you live far from here?' I asked.

He pointed through the window behind him.

'Let me show you,' he said. 'The farm you see from this window, it was all filled with trees. Over there is my old family home. And the one over there is my brother's new house. The other house over there is for my uncle. You see this one there, my other uncle. I'm living here. You see? I live upstairs and my office is downstairs.'

In the distance, chicken could be seen roaming near his old family home.

'So people here still raise chicken?' I asked.

'Yes, but I filed a complaint against my neighbours. My brother also lives upstairs. My cousins own shops here. We had a farm. We used to collect the fruit ourselves.'

'What did you grow on the farm?' I inquired.

'Like I told you, plums, grapes, peaches, and olives.'

'Apricots too?' I asked.

'And apricots. We also have a walnut tree in front of the house. It's been there ever since I was a child. You have to see it in the spring, when it's full of walnuts.'

Ever since he was thirteen years old, Jeries worked at his father's electrical appliance store and poultry shop in Fuheis. He also sold plums, peaches, and grapes from wooden boxes by the side of the road near his home to passers-by or drivers heading in and out of town. Then he tagged along with his uncle, a real estate agent, to show clients homes and land for sale. He put all the money he made towards household expenses his father was unable to cover.

After completing his army service, Jeries focused on his family's farm and managed a new flock of sheep his father had bought. 'I wanted to start a business after I served in the army but I couldn't afford it,' he said. 'I knew the only opportunity that was available to me was in public service.' He waited two years for his application to join the civil service to be processed. At twenty-three, he was finally given an interview.

'They called me and told me to come in for an interview and an exam. They told me there was an opening at the Civil Status and Passport Department.'

'What was the test like?' I asked.

A normal test. They asked us about Jordan, its borders and general matters really. So I did the interview and they told me, 'Okay, you can start work at the beginning of the following month.' I was happy. You know when you start a new job, you don't know anything about it. And there weren't any computers back then. Everything was done manually. We also had manual printers for the passports. So we worked, and the senior employees trained us. All the new employees are trained, trained to handle the files, on the counter, on how to deal with customers, printing, how to make a transaction, what documents are needed to complete a case, how to do such-and-such. I learned the job properly. At the beginning, I went to work every day from 8 a.m. to 2 p.m. and civil servants didn't take Saturdays off, only Fridays. Then the government made a so-called referendum. I remember a television station came to film us, to ask the employees whether people wanted to take Saturdays off in exchange for adding an extra hour per day. You know they were trying to show it's democratic, that the employees have a say, but the decision was already made, of course. So we took Saturdays off but worked until 3 p.m.

The public sector makes up more than 40 per cent of the labour force in Jordan. The system of employment goes back to the early years of the country's formation when the ruling regime ensured support among elite groups and tribes through patronage in the public sector. It is precisely for this reason that reform in this sector is not only perceived as an economic issue but as a politically sensitive one as well.

The country now has the largest public sector in the world proportionally to its population, according to a report published by the Jordanian government's Economic and Social Council. The sector, the authors of the report conclude, is 'inundated with red tape, low productivity, and *wasta* (favouritism) that hinder the country's competitiveness.' Although a clear majority of citizens believe that favouritism is a form of corruption, they also say it's necessary to obtain a job. Even today, Jordanians continue to seek jobs in public service because it is seen as a stable source of long-term employment. Yet, the long-term sustainability of the public sector without comprehensive reform remains questionable for many, even its long-term employees, like Jeries and others in his department.

THE DECIDER: JERIES AKROUSH

The private sector generally has longer working hours, lower average wages, and fewer benefits than the public sector. However, the pay for managerial positions in public service is almost 30 per cent lower than in the private sector, which makes it harder to attract those who would be required to run an effective and competitive public administration. As a manager with twenty-five years' experience in public service, Jeries receives around $600 a month. 'The employees are barely managing on their salaries,' said Jeries in December 2016. 'At the same time the public sector often hires more employees than it needs to. Debt is high in the country. How will it be fixed?'

Local municipalities are also weighed down by bloated bureaucracies and inadequate budgets. A recent decentralization law seeks to improve the performance and quality of services provided at the local district level.

One cold, grey afternoon in December 2016, Jeries invited me for lunch at his home to meet his family. When I arrived at the office below his apartment, Jeries introduced me to his older brother, Jehad, who is his partner at the real estate office. The glass front door was open and people seemed to just drop in and out. In that way, the office reminded me of the Civil Status and Passport Department.

When Jeries is away from the office, Jehad answers calls or takes clients to see plots and homes for sale. 'If you'll excuse me,' Jeries told Jehad and an old friend of theirs, a filmmaker who was sitting near the entrance.

Jeries walked out briskly and I followed. 'You see I always wanted to build this,' he said pointing to the window of his apartment, then down at the shops below. 'Before I built the home upstairs, I rented a small apartment across the street there. I took out a loan from the bank and began to build. Thanks to the real estate business, I made enough money to pay it back.'

We walked up two flights of stairs to the apartment, where Jeries' wife, Nancy, opened the door. She and Jeries sat together, surrounded by their four children, two girls and two boys. Jeries seated me next to his mother, Hikmat. 'Who do you know in Fuheis?' she asked me. Jordanians, especially elderly Jordanians, often converse about relatives or the town they come from. I named a few of my relatives who I knew lived in the area. She proceeded to name her parents, grandparents, and even distant relatives. She mentioned neighbours who had recently migrated to the United States.

Hikmat said she had a son who had moved to California more than eleven years ago but who still visits his family in Fuheis. Two years ago, Jeries had travelled there to spend Christmas with his brother. They had visited San Francisco, Las Vegas, and San Diego. 'It's so beautiful, isn't it?' he asked.

The conversation shifted from the state of the public sector in Jordan to the family recipe for homemade *jameed*, a traditional Jordanian specialty made with goat's milk and formed into balls of dry, hard yoghurt. The milk is kept in a woven cloth and churned to make these 'yoghurt rocks', then served with rice and meat.

Jeries led me to a quiet kitchen balcony overlooking an empty field. He told me he spent most of his time drinking coffee or having breakfast on the balcony in spring and summer. Another indoor balcony near the living room was sealed with white window frames. 'You see, this balcony is where we sit when it occasionally snows or it's really wet outside. We watch cars slide downhill,' he said, only half smiling. 'We watch the world go by from here because this is now the centre of town. Imagine, it used to be a dirt road and now look at what it has become.'

Adjacent to the indoor balcony was a long cabinet with a photograph of Jeries and his wife on their wedding day. A clear plastic bottle filled with mini chocolates obstructed the lower half of the photograph. In the background in the living room, the television was muted. Images from the war in Syria were flashing on the screen, as the ticker kept repeating the same news over and over.

THE DECIDER: JERIES AKROUSH

Next to the television was a small blue statue of the Virgin Mary with her arms outstretched. Near her stood a smaller statue of Jesus, looking ahead and surrounded by sheep. He wears a red robe and carries a lamb in one hand, holding it close to his chest.

Hikmat used to attend church regularly in Fuheis. Since she developed a problem with her legs, she attends less often. Nancy attends more regularly. Jeries is less religious than his parents and his wife, but insists on taking his family to church at Easter.

Jordan has some of the oldest Christian communities in the world; most of them belong to the Greek Orthodox Church, but there are also Catholics and Protestants. Many of the Christians in Jordan are descendants of ancient Arab tribes and fought together with Muslims against the Byzantines, the Crusaders, the Turks in the Great Arab Revolt, and more recently in the Arab-Israeli wars. However, the recent conflicts in the Middle East, specifically the rise of extremist groups like Al-Qaeda and ISIS, which have raised concern among many Muslims, have caused even more apprehensions among Christians like Jeries.

Christians in the country were few to begin with and we continue to see a high rate of migration. I think for the longest time they were emigrating for economic reasons, to find better opportunities, but now we feel it's gone beyond that. The region's future looks grim; people want to see a future for themselves and their families. The political instability and violence in the region just makes everyone feel uneasy. Just look at the entire Middle East these days. If I'm talking about Jordan, we must talk about how much the regional and political violence has impacted us in terms of spreading extremist ideology. Look at the Irbid cell, those terrorists who were captured by the police with weapons and explosives. There was the Hattar murder. There are more examples, but these incidents make citizens feel uneasy, that you can't take safety for granted.

The Hattar murder refers to the assassination of the prominent and controversial Jordanian writer Nahed Hattar. On

25 September 2016, the fifty-six-year-old was shot dead at close range by a Jordanian extremist at the steps of the capital's Palace of Justice. Hattar had been detained one month earlier after he posted a cartoon on Facebook that he had found online depicting a bearded man in heaven, smoking and in bed with two women, asking God to bring him wine and cashews. After receiving verbal attacks and death threats on social media, Hattar clarified that the cartoon he had shared was meant to illustrate the distorted religious views of Islamic State extremists, and not Islam. The murder of Hattar, who was from Fuheis, shocked the country and outraged many in his community.

The other incident to which Jeries alluded, the Irbid cell, was a March 2016 security operation, one of the largest of its kind in Jordan. It left seven suspected Islamic State militants and one security officer dead in the northern town of Irbid. Security officials said they had thwarted a plot by the militants to blow up civilian and military targets in the kingdom.

Also in the same year, I reported on a terrorist attack claimed by the Islamic State in the southern city of Karak, where seven Jordanian security officers, a Canadian tourist, and two Jordanian civilians were killed, and four attackers died in subsequent clashes. The assault began at an apartment where the terrorists were staying, before moving on to Karak's ancient crusader castle, a popular tourist destination in the city.

History and culture bring Jordanian Christians together with their Muslim neighbours. In 2003, it was Nancy's neighbour, a Muslim, who introduced her to her future husband Jeries. One day, Jeries' work colleague had asked him if he was engaged or married. Jeries was thirty-six years old at the time, and marriage was not on his mind. His colleague expressed dismay. It was a 'shame', she said, because her neighbour, Nancy, would be a perfect partner for him. He laughed off the idea, but agreed to meet her. He told me:

THE DECIDER: JERIES AKROUSH

One day I picked up my sister from work, as I always did, and we got in the car. She asked, 'Where are we going?' and I replied, 'I'm going to meet this lady.' So I went into Nancy's office and saw her. I said, 'Hello, how are you? I'm Jeries Akroush.' I think she was surprised. Nancy asked us what we wanted to drink. My sister said nothing; she clearly did not like the whole situation. I responded that I would like some water because my throat was dry, and some coffee without sugar, please. I added that my sister, Ragham, would also have some coffee. In the time we spent at Nancy's office, we didn't talk about anything major, just small talk, but I instantly took a liking to her, at first sight. I can't describe the feeling. I told her I would see her again soon. The following day I called the colleague who introduced us and asked for Nancy's phone number. She said, 'If you want to visit them at home, call her brother and arrange it with him,' and gave me his number. I called her brother and told him I was going to pass by the following evening and he said I was welcome. Nancy's family lived in Amman, not Fuheis. Then, after the phone call, it began to snow. I couldn't go. It was a bit surreal. I knew I wanted to be with her but I was also very honest. I said, 'Listen, Nancy, this is how I am: one, two, three. If you are fine with my character, then good.' I also told her, 'Sometimes I am forced to drop everything I am doing and show clients real estate or land, so I may be in the market with you and just leave you there and go.' Nancy said she appreciated my honesty. Then I told her father I needed to spend time with Nancy before I made any decision, and that's that.

Jeries and Nancy were married seventy-eight days later. Over the years, they had four children. In many ways, Jeries is impatient and traditionally patriarchal. His wife does all the housework. She makes sure their children complete their homework. When Nancy was working as a public servant, it was Jeries who asked her to quit her job after she had their second child. Jeries' mother admitted that her son was determined but short-tempered, even as a child. Sometimes he acknowledges that as well.

When I met Nancy for the first time in her apartment, I was curious to know what she had thought of Jeries the day he walked into her office. 'From the way he carried himself, I could tell he was confident,' she recalled. 'We spoke and he was naturally a very straightforward person, and proud. You don't find many people like that. We met briefly but my heart fluttered,' she said. 'Everything that happened, it just felt like it was meant to be.'

After Nancy had her first child, Malak (meaning 'angel' in Arabic), she continued to work as a public sector employee. Each morning, Jeries would drop Malak off at his mother's house, and Nancy would rush home at 3 p.m. to be with her. When they had their second child, Faheem (meaning 'perceptive'), Nancy was overwhelmed. Jeries' mother Hikmat used to take care of both children, who were close in age, when their parents were at work. Nancy would wake up at 5 a.m. every day. She cleaned the house. She prepared milk bottles. She cooked. She went to work.

Married women in Jordan are considerably less likely than unmarried women to participate in the labour force. Young and educated women face high levels of unemployment. The inability to integrate women into the workforce may be a major factor holding back economic growth in Jordan. Although Jeries had been the one to ask her to resign from work, Nancy confessed she was relieved. She was happy, she said, to dedicate all her time to her children. 'I know the hard work will pay off when they're older,' she said. 'If I raise them well, they will not become a burden later.'

When he became engaged to Nancy in February 2003, Jeries admitted he had $1,500 in his bank account. The 2003 Iraq war would transform his business. Iraqis fleeing from war and instability became the highest non-Jordanian investors in real estate in Jordan. They were looking for a safe place in the region to continue their businesses. Many of the refugees came from

Baghdad's middle or upper class, including businessmen, former government officials, doctors, and intellectuals. The demand raised the price of land and real estate, but more generally also fuelled inflation, helping Jeries' real estate business to boom. Jeries' work flow increased. Deals were made. The price of land where his clientele were based tripled in price and demand was high. Iraqis bought or built homes in affluent areas. Today there are even streets named after Baghdad and Basra.

In 2007, Jeries finally moved and expanded the office he works from today. Over the years, he paid off loans and moved into the apartment he now owns. In the past few years, however, Jeries has been echoing what he says many others in his business have pointed out: bureaucracy and red tape are turning some of his clients away.

The Jordan Housing Developers Association points out that a housing project, for example, must undergo seventeen different official procedures. The Greater Amman Municipality, which administers public and private construction, continues to impose strict restrictions and tedious bureaucratic procedures that Jeries fears will turn potential investors away. Indeed, investors have moved on to other countries, including the United Arab Emirates and Turkey, where there are simpler procedures and more explicit investment laws. The World Bank has suggested that fostering conditions for increased private investment and improved competitiveness will remain indispensable for Jordan to stimulate job creation and growth.

It had been a few weeks since I had last spoken with Jeries, so I called him on 13 February 2017. He told me that though he had been receiving calls and inquiries, the real estate business had recently been slowing down for him. After he finished work at the Civil Status and Passport Department, he had been spending his evenings playing cards with his relatives and friends in Fuheis.

The sluggish winter months also gave him the opportunity to travel. In December 2016, when I met Jeries at the passport department, he had just returned from a short trip to Beirut and Damascus. He mentioned restaurants where he had dined in Beirut and his apprehension before making the trip by car to Damascus. His cousin, who had travelled back and forth several times since the beginning of the civil war there, assured him that it would be safe. Jeries only told Nancy about the trip a day before. When she protested, he told her he was going anyway.

'There were many checkpoints on the way,' Jeries recalled. 'Somehow life in Damascus goes on. It's visibly a more depressing place than before the war. In the evening, the electricity is cut off from the streets but Syrians find a way to go on with their daily lives. Restaurants are busy, shops are still open. I still went to some of my favourite places there.'

Before the war, Damascus was an affordable getaway for many Jordanians. Only two hours away by car from Amman, it was a perfect place for families to spend their weekends. They would buy clothes, indulge in Syrian food, or stroll in the ancient *souks*. The war also halted cross-border trade when Jordan sealed its last official crossing point, after rebels seized control from government forces in 2015 on the Syrian side of the border crossing.

At the Civil Status and Passport Department, Jeries spoke more about his trip to his colleagues, who were surprised that he had gone and curious about conditions in Damascus. They reminisced about the visits they used to make there before the war. Outside his supervisor's office, employees were receiving applications, stamping papers, and issuing and renewing passports, turning some people away for missing paperwork. After he had finished updating his colleagues about his trip, Jeries walked to his office and, as was his habit, answered questions from clients or employees quickly and directly.

I asked Jeries if he agreed with a law that allowed only Jordanian men to pass their citizenship to their children, as well as to their wives, if they are foreign. Jordanian women are not able to bequeath citizenship to their children or spouses. In 2014, it was estimated that around 84,000 Jordanian women were married to foreign citizens in Jordan with nearly 34,000 children from these marriages. These children were only recently given access to some of the basic rights enjoyed by children with Jordanian nationality. Jeries said that the law, in his opinion, was necessary for now. The issue has been politicized by those who claim that providing citizenship to the population of Palestinian men married to Jordanian women would be a prelude to letting Palestinians settle permanently in Jordan. Some female politicians and critics from civil society organizations disagree with this argument and find the law discriminatory against women.

When I left the passport department, I recalled a brief encounter from the first time I had visited Jeries there. I had been approached by a young man who had followed me outside the department, holding a passport and some paperwork in his hand. 'Excuse me,' he had said. I turned around. 'I heard you speaking to Jeries. Forgive me for eavesdropping, but I just want to say his decisiveness and flexibility is welcomed by many here. He helped me finish all my paperwork quickly.' In offices around the country where a morning or even a day can be lost to filing paperwork and long queues, it was unusual, I thought, for someone to go out of their way to pay an employee a compliment.

When I met Jeries at his real estate office, after looking out at the walnut tree he pointed out from his window, I mentioned my encounter with the man outside the department. Jeries smiled his characteristic half-smile and interrupted me:

> Let me tell you why. I put myself in the person's shoes. I say, 'What if I was in that situation?' I would want someone to help me, not to complicate my life even more. If I know I can do something to help, I will do it. I am a manager; I have authority so I shouldn't hesitate to use it when I can. I'm employed in this position for there to be

less bureaucracy at the centre, to make decisions right then and there. Once, there was a lady who came to the office just as we were closing. She came to me and said, 'I must travel but I am missing some documents.' She showed me her plane ticket. I called the employee, he came from his home. We opened the office. I said, 'Okay, let's try to finish this.' You know why? Because I began to think about how she would have to cancel the ticket and it would be a problem.

Before lunch was served back at his home, I asked Jeries if he found his job as a public servant boring or tedious, especially after so many years. He said people often ask him the same question but he surprises them when he tells them he likes his work. His job as a bureaucrat does indeed follow a routine, but he continues to meet new people every day. He has made life-long friends at the department. Employees take turns buying everyone breakfast.

Jeries had witnessed a system transform due to digitization. He had uncovered attempts by individuals to forge identities. He is forced to be up to date on any change in rules and regulations that could impact thousands of citizens. By the end of 2017, he told me, Jordanians would need to exchange their old ID cards with smart IDs, which aimed to replace driving licenses, social security, and health insurance cards. By mid-2018, this change had come into effect, though the new IDs had not yet phased out driving licenses. The new ID cards integrated more information about the holder, with some data only being stored on the cards' electronic microprocessors, without being printed on the face of the cards.

Nancy was in the kitchen and Malak helped her bring out a large tray of *mansaf*. The chicken and meat were neatly spread over the yellow-tinged rice. The thick *jameed* yoghurt was served in a large bowl. Everyone took turns pouring the sauce over the rice and piling pine nuts onto their plate. The children picked the meat from the bones and mixed it with the sauce and rice. They took turns naming their favourite subjects at school: science, Arabic, social studies.

Nancy suddenly announced that despite being patriarchal, Jeries favoured his daughters over his sons. 'Unlike many Jordanian men, this is where he is different,' she explained. 'Still, I think he should be equal with them all. I love all my children the same.' Her children looked at her attentively and then at their father. When Malak was born thirteen years ago, her father had made sure there was celebratory gunfire. Traditionally in Jordan, it is the arrival of a male child that is hailed and celebrated. After Malak's baptism ceremony, Jeries had invited family and friends to a big party with loud music and plenty of food. 'Bigger than my wedding party,' he said.

I felt I was overstaying my welcome. I could see Jeries was becoming anxious. He was smoking more frequently and his body was inching closer to the edge of the couch. Every time I tried to excuse myself, the family would ask me to wait. There were fruits—pomegranates, persimmon, oranges. Then there was coffee. After a brief silence, Jeries raised his small cup and said, 'It's without cardamom. Plain. Just the way I like it.'

6

THE REBEL READER

LINA ASAAD

It was a Facebook post that had got Lina into trouble at school, and that now had her all riled up in between sips of fruit-flavoured iced tea. 'We have girls at school who are such attention seekers,' she said, with an emphasis on the word 'such'.

Lina related how one day she had come out of class to find her school bag was gone. In the distance, she saw her books scattered on the ground and her notebook pages ripped out. When she and her friends had complained to the principal, nothing was done. Her friend's sister took to Facebook. She wrote about the incident and the lack of action from the principal, and tagged the school in her post.

'Then it got crazy,' Lina explained when we first met in February 2017 at a speciality tea café, as live turtles swam in glass tanks overlooking graffiti-covered cement barriers to protect the entrance of The British Council on Rainbow Street. The next day, Lina's mother had been called into the principal's office. The administration was furious, convinced that Lina had written the Facebook post. 'The principal wanted me to confess,' explained Lina, 'but after two hours, everyone there realized it wasn't me. Still, the point is that the administration took an online post more seriously than my bag being stolen and finding who was responsible.'

This is Lina's world at fifteen years old: social media, school, best friends, and books. In some ways, she is a typical student attending public school in East Amman, except that she speaks her mind often, and when she saves money, she buys books.

A quarter of children in the Middle East and North African region are not enrolled in school or have fallen two grades behind. According to a 2017 UNICEF report, lack of education was found to be a key driver of inequality and poverty for children. Still, Arab youth in general have higher literacy rates than in the past and are more connected to the world through the internet.

During the protests, there was a focus on the role of social media and mobile phones as means for collective activism online and offline, as alternatives to state-owned media channels for spreading news. The use of social media platforms more than doubled in Arab countries during the protests, except in Libya, according to the 2011 Arab Media Social Report. Nine out of ten Egyptians and Tunisians responded to the same poll stating that they used Facebook to organize protests and spread awareness. At the time, young Egyptians referred to themselves as 'the Facebook generation'.

Today, amateur videos, blogs, photo-sharing platforms, emails, and text messages are still being used across the Middle East, including in Syria and Iraq, to record and share news of atrocities and torture perpetrated by regimes, extremists and opposition groups. However, governments in the region have since legislated to limit what can be said online.

Lina has one foot in Jordan, in the Arab world, and the other foot somewhere else. That other place is perhaps best exemplified by the music she listens to, including Mashrou' Leila, a

Lebanese alternative rock band that found a regional audience during the Arab Spring. As Elias Muhanna wrote in the *New Yorker*, the group has songs 'about quotidian life in Beirut: busybody gossip about couples on the boardwalk, the bored soldier hassling young men at a checkpoint, the social pressure to marry someone from your own sect.'

In 2016, Mashrou' Leila was barred from entering Jordan, days before a scheduled concert in Amman's Roman amphitheatre. The city's then mayor was quoted in the *Jordan Times* as saying that the group's songs and lyrics 'do not comply with the nature of Jordanian society.' The ban was lifted following widespread international media coverage and public outcry from fans, but the band, fronted by openly gay lead singer Hamed Sinno, announced they still would not perform as planned. They had been unofficially informed, according to a post on their Facebook page, that they would not be allowed to perform in future because of 'our political and religious beliefs and endorsement of gender equality and sexual freedom.'

A year later, the musicians were once again prevented from performing in Jordan, despite obtaining the necessary permits, including the support of the ministry of tourism. Their concert was cancelled following a pronouncement by the ministry of the interior. The decision spurred a heated online debate by Jordanians, and exchanges of strong words, both in support of and against the group. Mashrou' Leila released a statement on its Facebook page:

> Pretending that these oppressive decisions are necessary under the guise of protecting 'Jordanian customs and traditions' frames traditions in a horribly regressive light ... Again, one has only to look at the reaction of the Jordanian people to the cancellation, to see that the notion of a singular, homogeneous society that shares these 'customs and traditions,' does not seem to apply to Jordanian people, much as it cannot apply to anyone and anywhere else.

Indeed, Lina and her friends encapsulate the diversity of tastes and opinions in Jordan. As well as Mashrou' Leila, Lina also listens to Jadal—a Jordanian rock band—Canadian singer The Weeknd, and the American singer Melanie Martinez. 'Her song 'Cry Baby' is my absolute favourite,' she wrote to me on Instagram. She also admires the singer, songwriter and actor Troye Sivan, an Australian who was born in South Africa.

Before I met Lina, I knew little about social media influencers from the Arab region and beyond. I realized it was important to familiarize myself with some of the names she mentioned often during our conversations. They were her role models, she noted, and their online world was where she spent most of her time after school.

> Connor Franta, he's a movie maker and content creator, he's inspiring. He just released a book, *Note to Self*. Then there's Tyler Oakley, he's a social media star and influencer and wrote the book *Binge*. Ben J. Pierce is also a content creator on YouTube, but Connor is kind of more artistic than Ben, who often does comedy videos and make-up tutorials. Why don't you look him up? There's Omar Farooq from Bahrain who makes short films. There's Fly With Haifa, she's Palestinian but lived in the Emirates. I love her content a lot, it's different and creative. She encourages me to be myself and to do what makes me happy.

To the dismay of her teachers, Lina often skips the morning school routine: standing in line, singing the national anthem, listening to Quranic verses, answering trivia questions, and participating in light physical exercises. When she's not at school, Lina wears brightly coloured hijabs, glasses, and Converse-like shoes. If students do choose to wear a hijab in public school, it has to be white.

Lina lives in an area called Al-Hashmi Al-Shamali in eastern Amman that hosts Iraqis, Syrians, Palestinians, and Jordanians. It is distinctly not fancy. Rent is affordable, and it is here that one can arguably find the working class living—carpenters, salespersons, mechanics, public school teachers.

Lina lives with her parents and three siblings in a three-bedroom apartment with a windowless living room adjoining a more formal seating area where the family receives guests. Her home is near a market, mainly filled with shops selling office stationery, shoes, mobile phones, baby products, and a bakery with a bright neon sign. There is also a dentist's office, and a number of dusty white and beige apartments that look like faded Lego blocks.

When I met Lina's parents at their home, Nabeela, her mother, proudly presented me with a folder that included her daughter's childhood drawings, certificates, and school reports. She sifted through the pile. 'These are Lulu's things,' she said fondly, using Lina's nickname.

> This is a picture of her and her classmates in Syria. Here is a certificate, they honoured her at school there. This was the first thing she ever wrote to me. I saved it. Can you read her handwriting? It says: 'To Mum, I love you. Your name is carved in my heart and God bless you.'

Lina and her siblings have been living in Al-Hashmi Al-Shamali all their lives, except in 2008 when Qasem, their father, worked at an upscale hotel in Damascus and decided to take his family with him for one year. In 2010–11, they had also briefly lived in Khobar in Saudi Arabia, where he had worked in a hotel. The children had attended school there for one semester.

Qasem was born and raised in Kuwait, while Nabeela was born in Amman and raised in Saudi Arabia. Both are Jordanians of Palestinian origin and came to Jordan in 1990, although they did not know each other then. Qasem arrived in Jordan during one of the largest displacements of Palestinians from any Arab state. In 1990, the Palestinian Liberation Organization and its former leader, Yasser Arafat, aligned themselves with Saddam Hussein, who had invaded Kuwait earlier that year. In retaliation for that alliance, hundreds of thousands of Palestinians with Jordanian citizenship were evicted from Kuwait and consequently fled to Jordan. The economy in Jordan was already strained and Palestinians who arrived became resentful because of the jobs, homes, and lives they were forced to leave behind.

Qasem and Nabeela were married in 1995. They both work hard; the only times Nabeela has taken a break from working were when the family lived in Damascus and Khobar. She had known they would only be there temporarily, and had wanted to spend more time with her children.

Today Nabeela works as a nurse at the burns and cosmetic restoration unit at one of the largest and oldest public hospitals in the country. Qasem is head of housekeeping at an upscale hotel in Amman and is used to working long hours. When we met at their home one evening in March 2017, Qasem was still wearing his suit and was stretching his neck sideways, clearly having just arrived from work. Lina sat on the couch with her legs crossed, wearing a bright orange hijab, in between her father and her older sister Manal, who had also joined us at the café the first time we met.

'There are things we discovered about Lina that we didn't know at first,' explained Nabeela as she brought out a tray with red berry juice and another crammed with chocolates and nuts—cashews, roasted almonds, peanuts. 'We thought Lina was quiet and shy, but it turned out she's not. I mean she still gets a bit shy, but that doesn't keep her from being creative and outspoken.'

Although her parents spoke mostly about their own lives, their careers and the war in Syria, Lina insisted twice on interjecting. The first time was when Nabeela described Lina's personality, and the second when I asked her parents about their daughter's future.

'The special thing about Lina is when she sets her mind on something she gets it done. When she insists on something ...'

'So she's persistent?' I asked.

'Yes. Even in school if she wasn't doing well, she would say, "I am going to get a high grade." She would do whatever it takes, even if she needed to stay up all night studying for three or four days. If she wants to do something, she does it. That's it.'

'I still cause drama,' Lina joked.

'You like drama?' I asked.

'Only at school, because of the people there.'

'And at home too,' her mother corrected.

When I met Lina, I was impressed by her English language skills. Her language teacher had once asked her a question in front of the class to which Lina couldn't respond. After that incident, she had spent hours learning English, mainly through films, music, and YouTube. She didn't just want to improve, she said, but to excel. 'The school didn't help me out at all with my English, so I depended on myself.'

Some Jordanian parents believe that being proficient in English provides their children with better educational and work opportunities, yet English instruction continues to deteriorate in public schools, according to local and international data. Lina's family had often watched documentaries in English when she was young. When they had lived in Saudi Arabia, Qasem had been afraid his children would forget the language because it was not taught at the school they attended there, so he only spoke with his children in English at home. Today, Lina has surpassed her peers in English class and often helps them with their homework.

When I first met Lina, she was planning to compete in the Arab Reading Challenge along with two other students. The competition was launched in 2015 by Dubai's ruler, Sheikh Mohammed bin Rashid, to encourage youth to read Arabic books. Estimates vary on general readership in the region but according to Mohamed Hashem, director of a Cairo publishing house, the Arab world suffers from a 'reading crisis'. Lack of reliable book production and sales, low readership, censorship, weak distribution, and piracy continue to hold the region back.

For students to compete in the challenge, they must read and summarize fifty books in Arabic. If they are selected, they are then asked a series of questions by a panel of judges. Lina listed many of the books she read, most of them translated into Arabic from English—*The Alchemist*, *Eat Pray Love*, *The Forty Rules of Love*. To her disappointment, she later discovered that because of a bureaucratic mishap, she was not officially registered to compete.

Between 1980 and 2002, adult literacy rates for Jordanian women rose from 55 per cent to 86 per cent. Education in Jordan is compulsory from first grade to tenth grade, and all students are entitled to free education in public schools. For students who continue, marks from eighth to tenth grade are used to determine if they are better suited to the humanities or scientific track, and dictate what they are eligible to apply for. Lina enjoys chemistry and biology, but not physics and maths, so she is unlikely to end up in the scientific stream, a more prestigious course in the eyes of society. At the end of twelfth grade, students are required to take a rigorous and comprehensive examination, which essentially decides their fate: whether they can pursue higher education, and what majors they can choose from.

The public school system mainly continues to encourage rote learning, rather than fostering critical thinking. It also has poorly trained teachers as well as limited use of technology. A gap between the educational system and job market requirements contributes considerably to unemployment among both men and women. One problem for women is that they tend to concentrate on studying the humanities, which do not necessarily teach the skills employers are seeking. Education reform is much discussed in Jordan, including plans to encourage students to enrol in practical vocational training rather than in the academic stream, but little has come of these discussions so far.

THE REBEL READER: LINA ASAAD

Although Jordan's higher education system is well regarded in the region, a significant percentage of unemployed Jordanians hold a secondary or higher certificate, according to the World Bank. Many women graduates also face family, social, and mobility constraints, which limit their opportunities. This is more severe if the women live in more rural and socially conservative areas where simply going to training sessions outside the home, for example, can cause family feuds. For other women, lack of transportation from rural districts to Amman is a barrier.

While young women like Lina and her sister Manal display a lot of enthusiasm toward education and employment, in actual fact, both men and women in Jordan can spend a long time searching without finding a job, leading them to drop out of the labour market. In some Arab countries, including Jordan, the more educated the women are, the less of a chance they have of finding a job.

'They also force a woman to choose between her children and her job,' said Nabeela as the family began debating the role of women in the workplace.

'Besides that, they are underpaid, especially compared to men with the same job,' added Qasem.

'They are underappreciated,' Lina chimed in.

'Exactly,' Nabeela said.

'That's why I want to study mass communications, because I can begin my career from scratch, especially in filmmaking and directing,' announced Lina.

'She's insisting on mass media and communications,' said Qasem.

'I started taking online courses. I also began to develop my photography skills. I took video editing a long time ago, three years ago, when I knew I wanted to pursue a career in media.'

'So you're self-teaching, just like you taught yourself English?' I asked.

'Yes, and it really helped me develop my skills. My aim is first to go to a university here to study mass media and communications, and then to work until I make enough money to go to Abu Dhabi where they have a New York University campus, or maybe to New York itself to study filmmaking.'

Her mother looked concerned.

'I worry about my children a lot,' Nabeela said.

'Come on, don't say no,' Lina said forcefully. 'You see? She's saying no.'

'I didn't say no,' her mother replied. 'We'll see.'

'It has to be an investment, what they study,' said Qasem. 'At the end of the day if Lina studies mass media and communications, will she get a return on that here in Jordan? That's where the challenge lies. But it's entertaining and could present something new for her every day. Still ... will it be useful for her? We don't force them and in the end they will make their own decisions.'

'We just guide them,' explained Nabeela.

I accompanied Lina to school one early morning in March 2017. It had rained heavily the night before but by the time I arrived at Lina's building the few scattered showers had stopped and the grey sky was turning pale blue. I waited in the car, in front of rows of apartment buildings with doors. Olive trees lined the pavement near her home and in amongst them a fig tree stood out, its leaves just beginning to grow.

A white and orange striped cat slipped into an open gate. A girl with pigtails on her way to school threw a plastic bag in one of the three large aluminium dumpsters on the street. Another white and black spotted cat crossed the road and squeezed through a small opening in the gate of an apartment building. The only commotion on the street at 6.45 a.m. was caused by school buses, students, and Egyptian day labourers who were buying tea from a tiny coffee stand on their way to work.

THE REBEL READER: LINA ASAAD

Lina came downstairs, seemingly dazed, and waved to me. We had gone only a few steps across the street before her two friends, Danya and Tala, met us. Lina had been awake since 2.30 a.m. studying for a maths exam, and the three discussed it as we walked. On the way, the girls stopped at a bakery to pick up a croissant filled with white cheese, then went to the shop next door for a small bag of falafel. They stuffed the croissant with pieces of falafel and ate as they walked. We passed two school administrators, but neither exchanged greetings. Lina and her friends often stop to buy tea, but on that day, they chose not to. There were a few young men congregating in front of the shop, and the girls told me they felt uncomfortable.

When we arrived at the school, empty crisps packets covered most of the pavement, and a stream of students, all female, flooded through the school gates. I was met by Lina's Arabic teacher, Wafa, who led me to the principal's office so I could obtain permission to attend classes with Lina that day.

Wafa pointed to the front playground, where the students were forming lines for the morning assembly that Lina and her friends often skipped. She walked me to the back of the school where there was a small library, computer lab, and science lab, none of which were open. The principal met us in the hallway and talked to me angrily about the double-shift school system in which every class was only half an hour. She also spoke about the school's lack of funds for reconstruction and lack of utilities.

Suddenly, Lina ran towards us panicked. 'Oh my God, we have an exam now,' she announced and then dashed back into the class. The maths exam took the students over an hour to complete, and because each class was only half an hour, English had been cancelled that day.

The classroom had thirty-one students, and nearly all of them wore white hijabs. Two students in the classroom were Syrians; the rest were Jordanian. Lina wore a green jacket, glasses and a white hijab, with jeans under the green apron of her school uniform.

The students kept their jackets on in class. It was chilly and there was no heating, just a ceiling fan. Lina told me that on colder days, the teacher would bring a portable heater to the class. Although they wore a uniform, the students were free to choose their shoes. Most of them wore trainers; Lina's were neon Nikes, blue and fuchsia pink, with a neon green stripe near the ankle. Most of the students carried multi-coloured school bags as well—purple, yellow, striped magenta.

On the classroom wall were an Arabic grammar poster and one with a list of words inside a picture of a honeycomb. Another poster had the names and corresponding pictures of the five senses. There were two posters in English including one that read: 'Door, Table, Clock, Chair, Classroom'. A small peach and yellow cabinet obstructed a view of the rest of the poster's words.

'You need more time?' asked the English teacher, who was roaming around the classroom. In the drawers of the worn-out desks were more crisp packets, empty juice cartons stuffed inside. Some students had pencil cases; others had only pencils and rubbers. Another teacher came into the class: 'I said I didn't want you to write in blue ink.' She then asked one of the students to move to another desk.

Because of the two-shift schedule, classes begin at 7 a.m. and end at noon, when classes begin for another batch of younger students. Lina's lessons felt hurried: geometry and algebra, Islamic religion, science, and Arabic. The students excitedly told their Islamic studies teacher, who was wheelchair-ridden and assisted by a teenager into the classroom, that they had prepared activities. They played musical chairs; the one who was left out had to answer a question from the textbook. The teacher played music she had saved on her mobile phone.

Then the students took turns puffing away a mountain of flour from a plate to find a folded piece of paper inside with a question that was read aloud and answered in front of the class. They also took turns popping balloons with similar questions hidden inside. There was excitement in the air, and the atmosphere felt festive.

The teacher interrupted the game and told the class she had to explain the lesson before they could continue with the rest of the games. The students hurried back to their desks and opened their textbooks. The teacher began to explain the difference between dialogue and argument. 'Arguing for the sake of arguing is egotistic, it's arguing just for the sake of winning, but then there is dialogue which is so much more constructive,' she told the students. 'Okay, now who can quickly memorize the *hadith* in the textbook and say it aloud to the rest of the class?'

The students looked down at the *hadith*, or saying of the Prophet Muhammad. Several repeated the paragraph over and over to themselves and then a student in the first row raised her hand and recited it word for word. The teacher praised her and continued with the lesson, going on to lecture the class about God's punishment for lying and about the virtue of being humble. 'When you lie, what happens?' she asked the students, who looked down at their textbooks and then eagerly raised their hands. A student in the middle row answered, 'You lose credibility.'

After religion class came science. When the teacher entered the class, the mood shifted. She was stern and serious. She spoke about carbon, hydrogen and oxygen, mushrooms and bacteria. I sat on the sole spare seat, part of a two-seat worn-out bench, next to a student named Bisan. She allowed me to share her science textbook to follow the lesson. During the brief break after science, the students disappeared and came back quickly. Bisan offered me a bag of crisps and when I declined, she said, 'Please, I got it especially for you.'

The last class that day was Arabic. It began with one student, who looked like she had barely slept the night before, stuffing crisps in her mouth when the teacher was not looking. The teacher wrote Arabic verbs on the board, past and present tenses.

When one of her students answered a question incorrectly, Wafa joked, 'When you eat falafel, your brain seems to shut down.' Everyone laughed. Lina passed a note to Danya.

When classes were over, I took the opportunity to ask the students about their challenges as female teenagers in Jordan, but also what they felt was positive about their lives. Lina raised her hand and said that as young women, they yearned for more freedom. They wanted to go to places that only their brothers were allowed to go. Another student said she wanted to learn languages that were not offered in their school, like French. Other students said they wanted the school to include more time for arts and crafts; others wanted the school to focus more on physical education. At the time, the class had no regular P.E. teacher, so the session was usually cancelled.

Compared to the state of war raging in neighbouring countries, the students said they felt safe in Jordan. They were aware that living in a war zone or being a refugee meant an interruption in education. The Syrian students looked down at their desks and nodded. Others said that compared to other countries in the region, they felt the academic curriculum in Jordan was strong. Many agreed; a few disagreed. Some students said they felt they had made lifelong friendships with some of their teachers.

Arabic class ended early that day, but already students from the second shift (first to sixth grade), which included both girls and boys, roamed in the playground and in the hallways. Since Lina's class finished early, Wafa told her students to wait in the front yard until the bell rang. They huddled together with their schoolbags, forming a semicircle, waiting. 'There is life skills training at a centre near my home and it's free of charge,' said one student from Lina's class. 'My parents do not allow me to go there because there are boys. We miss out on a lot of opportunities like that,' she told me.

We left the school premises as soon as the bell rang and I walked on the main market road with Lina and five of her friends. They stopped when they saw the open back of a blue van packed with plants for sale, each of them placed in a small black plastic bag filled with soil. A few of the students, including Lina, stopped and bought plants with mint leaves. Lina then announced that they were going to stop to buy ice cream because it was finally warm outside. As she walked she pointed out a few shops that had been there since she was a child. The friends discussed their plans for the weekend; one was going to visit her grandparents, another was going to the mall. Lina planned to spend her time watching television. 'Oh you know, like the ones on Netflix,' she said. 'I watch shows like *Black Mirror*, *Stranger Things*, *Pretty Little Liars*, and with Manal sometimes I watch *Grey's Anatomy*.'

When we arrived at the ice cream shop and Lina turned around to take her cone, I noticed two small pins stuck on the top of her bag. One was a cactus plant and the other was a shiny American flag.

> I have the cactus pin because, as you may have already noticed, I love plants. I had a cat pin too but it fell off; I had it because I love cats. And I have this American flag because it looks nice and it reminds me of my dream of going to film school in New York.

7

NOMAD AT HEART

SULTAN AL-MAZNAH

He still owns camels. He loves to gaze at the stars and to wander the desert on foot for hours. Sultan Al-Maznah is a nomad at heart, a Bedouin, but he has chosen to abandon a tent for a cement home, a bucket of water for a shower head, and fire for electricity.

Sultan lives in a peach-painted cement house in Manshieh, a southern provincial village surrounded by the spectacular rose-coloured mountains and sandstone cliffs of Wadi Rum. During the day, the sun is bright and intense. It bears down harshly on the shiny, soft sand and there is little shade. The valley has been inhabited by many peoples with many cultures, including the Nabateans who built the famous archaeological city of Petra, a UNESCO world heritage site in Jordan dating back to around 300 BC. Wadi Rum's desert is vast and protected by the government's camel-riding mountain security, the Desert Force.

While Sultan and his parents' generations try to hold on to their identity and traditions, the reach of technology and tourism constantly forces them to adapt and change. Sultan still eats lentils, beans, and sardines, but more recently his favourite meal has been fried chicken. Life for him is unthinkable without his camels, but he drives a pickup truck.

Wadi Rum is often called the desert of Lawrence of Arabia, after T. E. Lawrence, a British officer and author of *Seven Pillars of Wisdom*, an account of his time with the British army during World War I. Lawrence described the area as 'vast, echoing, and God-like.' He spent time here and found fame and affinity among the Arab Bedouin tribes, many of whom still exist here today. Some tribes that took up arms with Lawrence against the Ottomans continue to live in Wadi Rum today.

On the main road to Manshieh is Wadi Rum's visiting centre, a large modern building with several outdoor shops shaded by white awnings. There are stones carved or spray-painted with the name 'Howeitat', a prominent Jordanian tribe that includes Sultan's mother and her family. A natural water aquifer, Lawrence's Spring, is also named after the young British soldier, who washed there according to local lore. In 1917, Lawrence, with the help of several Arab tribes, captured Jordan's southern town of Aqaba, close to the Saudi border, from the Turks, who were desperately seeking to hold on to the Ottoman Empire.

When the emirate of Transjordan was created in 1921 by the British mandate, there were nearly 400,000 inhabitants in the country, many of them farmers, shepherds, and tribespeople in villages and towns. While the ruler at the time, Emir Abdullah I, administered in the manner of a tribal leader, the British handled government affairs. In exchange for the tribes' loyalty, Emir Abdullah, who went on to become king in 1946, offered the Bedouins land and built them into the system and structure of the state by offering them security and army positions. Sultan, who is twenty-two years old, serves in the Jordanian Armed Forces and is an example of that existing structure.

I was convinced that the best place to work was in the military. At least it's guaranteed work. You receive a monthly salary. It's not like in tourism where you have work today but maybe none tomorrow. I also like to serve my country, and I like being a soldier. What made me like it even more is that when you retire after twenty years, your pension is guaranteed for the rest of your life. After you die, the pension goes to your family. The army preserves your rights. If you don't work in the army, you end up paying for your children's college tuition. When I have kids, I will educate them and I won't have to pay for it—the military will. I'm now stationed near my home too.

Sultan has a slight frame and small, dark brown eyes that disappear from his face when he smiles. The young soldier often wears the traditional *dishdasha*, an ankle-length garment with long sleeves. For the first year and a half of his life, he lived with his parents in a tent in the desert. Then his father built a concrete room and erected the tent next to it. Eventually, additional rooms were built, including a kitchen, and the tent was removed.

Sultan has nine siblings, but is the eldest male in the family and has worked nearly all his life. For Bedouin parents and their children, access to education nowadays is important but working and developing skills that match the limited employment opportunities available are even more vital. For the most part, the general lack of investment and the absence of private sector interest in rural villages like Manshieh dissuades young people from pursuing higher degrees.

When he attended school as a child, the young Bedouin would spend his afternoons in Wadi Rum with tourists who rode his camel in exchange for a fee. The attacks on 11 September 2001 in the United States and the Arab Spring have combined to stem the flow of tourists to places like Jordan and to many other countries in the Arab world. The lack of visitors has forced the Bedouin population to seek other means to survive. Ten years ago, Sultan's father used his savings to open a one-room store to sell fuel. A year later, he converted it into a small grocery shop on the side of his home. 'As far back as I can remember,' recalled Sultan nonchalantly, 'I was always working.'

I worked in the grocery shop for a while. Before that I used to wake up some days at 5.30 a.m. and stay out until 7.30 p.m., spending all day exploring nature and monuments with the tourists, of course. I spent approximately two years working in tourism. The industry sometimes has low points, like now, it's very slow.

I visited the family's hometown, a village near Diseh, located northwest of Wadi Rum, an area less frequented by tourists. As I approached in my car, Bedouin women crossed the one-lane main road leading to the village, herding sheep and newborn goats: black, grey, and white. Framed by dizzying mountains, the area was a blanket of red sand over which reigned a serene silence. There was little else, aside from a few green bushes, purple flowers, pebbles and rocks, caves carved in the towering mountains, and a railroad track next to the road. Camels were transported in the back of pickup trucks or grazed freely in the middle of the desert.

Unlike the deserts of Wadi Rum, an aquifer led Bedouins to settle in Diseh, which is visibly more green, supporting palm and olive trees, shrubs, and plants. As a child, Sultan attended public school there but his mother, Eideh, described how he got into fights, refused to listen to his teachers, and hardly took his school work seriously.

'School wasn't the only thing on my mind,' explained Sultan as he drove his pickup through the desert one afternoon in March 2017. 'After the school day ended, I would go back home and then quickly go out again to work. I always felt I had other responsibilities and I didn't concentrate on studying.'

In his third year at the school, his father moved him to Prince Hussein bin Abdullah School, an all-male military academy, where he became more disciplined. The school is within walking distance from his home, near Diseh's main market with its eclectic collection of stores selling fruit and vegetables, dairy products, poultry, mobile phones, haberdashery, Saudi products and accessories, and car parts, as well as a mosque, the village's visiting centre, and a hostel with a sign that read 'Rum Magic Camp.'

Although he enjoyed studying at the military school, the young Bedouin dropped out four years later. Tourism was picking up again and he began earning more money.

> I finished my first semester of seventh grade and then worked during the winter holidays; tour guides were making good money, so it was tempting. You did what you wanted and earned money at the same time. It made you feel older than your years. When I began working in the tourism sector, thank God I was earning money on a daily basis, and I saw that it was something that I could really benefit from and that would help my family too. I thought if I continued studying in grade seven, eight, nine, then I wouldn't get a chance to build a life of my own. During those four years, I worked hard and I felt like I made it. I bought a car and built a house, the house we are living in now. I also went to work as a guard for a Turkish company. If I had continued studying all the way to college, it would have been difficult for me to get married, to find work, build myself up, but at twenty-one years old, I got married and now can provide everything and help my family as well.

When we met in March 2017, Sultan's duty as a soldier was to guard the military school building he had once attended, with its white steel window frames and a fluttering Jordanian flag. The words 'Sound Mind, Sound Body' were written on the school wall behind a fenced football field where Sultan used to practice. Further afield was a camel race track where his own camels had once competed.

Unlike in other cities and towns across the country, the community here is tight-knit. Tribes know each other; they leave their camels to graze freely in the desert, sometimes for days, knowing the prized animals will be safe. Sultan's parents own five camels and two rabbits, and they once had a large flock of sheep and goats that his mother used to tend. Although Bedouins are traditionally conservative, women play a major role in household affairs. They herd sheep and goats, milk the animals, cook, and sew clothes.

Young men I talked to admitted that some Bedouin women nowadays will only accept a marriage proposal if they are guaranteed a concrete home. Living in a tent is no longer desirable because of the lack of resources and harsh conditions. Both men and women are also using social networking platforms to view trends, exchange news and communicate.

'What our mothers and grandmothers had to endure is no longer acceptable to the younger generation,' explained Sultan. 'Most people also have smartphones; they have television access and see what is out there.'

The Bedouin women I met spend weekdays in the main villages where markets, services, and schools are located. The women who do have jobs are mainly employed in the public sector or as school teachers. On weekends they can be found in the desert. Families like Sultan and his wife go camping, or visit elders and family members still living in tents and in rural areas.

Traditionally, women also weave the black tents that are often seen from a distance in the desert. The tents are called *beit shaer*, literally a 'house of hair'; they are woven from goat hair and often include two main sections. The public area for receiving guests is encircled by mattresses and pillows arranged around the centre, which is used for serving tea and coffee beside a fire. Unlike in more urban and conservative areas across Jordan, Bedouin women sometimes join in the conversations, even in the presence of men who are not relatives. The second section of the tent includes the kitchen and a more private area for the family, especially for the women.

The first day I arrived in Manshieh, Sultan was on duty, which delayed our meeting to the following day. Sultan's brother, Mohammad, took me on a tour of their home and proudly intro-

1. Sultan Al-Maznah serves in the Jordanian Armed Forces in a system established by King Abdullah I, who offered positions in the army to Bedouin tribesmen in exchange for their loyalty.

2. Sultan with some of his family's camels. Bedouin tribes know and trust each other—they leave their camels to graze freely in the desert, sometimes for days, knowing the prized animals will be safe.

3. Sultan with his father, standing near their home in Manshieh, a southern Jordanian provincial village surrounded by the spectacular rose-coloured mountains and sandstone cliffs of Wadi Rum.

4. Lina Asaad at home with her family.

5. Lina in her bedroom.

6. Lina with her school friends.

7. Shirene Rifai at home with her family.

8. Shirene in her upscale West Amman neighbourhood, Um Uthaina, standing in front of luxury store Chopard, which she has promoted as a social media influencer.

9. Shirene and two of her friends posing as models for Mother's Day.

10. Jamal Shultaf in front of his apartment building in the working-class suburb Chicago Ridge, Illinois.

11. Jamal brings his family to a park near their home in Chicago Ridge. 'When we come here, we forget about any hardship,' he said.

12. Jamal at work as a waiter at Al Bawadi Grill, a Middle Eastern restaurant in Chicago.

13. Sawsan Maani with her family.

14. Sawsan relaxing and smoking *argeeleh*.

15. Sawsan with her husband, Ahmad Jaber. Sawsan and Ahmad were married on 4 August 1989 and have eight children.

16. Sawsan with her two grandchildren and other family members in the background. Her family lives in Marj Al-Hamam, a neighbourhood south of Amman.

duced me to their five camels. The concrete room where Ibraheem, their father, receives guests is equipped with a heater, windows, a television, a carpeted floor, and several mattresses. Whenever I visited him there was a *dalleh* nearby, a large pot filled with hot sweet tea, next to several small cups resembling oversized thimbles.

Mohammad had just returned home from the same military school his brother Sultan had attended when he was younger. The fourteen-year-old said he was being offered a job as a guard and was considering leaving school. 'Our financial situation doesn't allow us for him to miss a work opportunity; I would have him leave school for a good job,' Ibraheem told me. The guest room was furnished with red carpets, and a television on mute was displaying images from the war in Syria. 'That's how it is here. The reality is we're living in remote areas without proper facilities, infrastructure or institutions,' he said. 'People with degrees can't find jobs here, they have to go to Aqaba or the bigger cities and even then, young men can't find jobs. It's even harder for women.'

Mohammad took me to visit their cousin, Ali Al-Maznah, who appeared from a tent wearing a golden brown *dishdasha*. He stood in front of the family's five camels that I had met earlier, with one hand in his pocket and the other holding a mobile phone. Ali graduated from school and is a technician working in the Civil Defense Directorate in Amman. He visits his family every weekend, despite the three-and-a-half-hour journey each way. 'I like the city but I love the sand, the mountains, the moon and the stars here,' he said as he prepared to return to Amman the following morning. Although his family lives in a large tent, they had also built a private room to sleep in and for warmth in the winter months.

I asked Ibraheem if we could meet a family that had refused to build a cement home or abandon their nomadic way of life.

Ibraheem drove me and his youngest son, Abood, in his pickup truck in the desert for nearly half an hour. With the help of his ancestral knowledge of the area, he navigated the desert effortlessly, despite there being no vehicle tracks, signs, dirt roads, or any distinguishable features except varied mountain elevations. The pickup truck stopped near a Bedouin family, the grandparents and uncles of Sultan's wife, Nisreen. They were moving their belongings, packing up parts of their tent and placing them into the back of a pickup truck. We followed them. Only a short distance away, they were setting up the rest of the tent. Scarcity of water and the search for pastoral land force Bedouins to move frequently.

A spotted dog belonging to the family, mainly used for protection and herding, followed the pickup truck and barked until the vehicle stopped. We stepped inside the tent and were greeted by both Bedouin men and women. Three young men had stopped by while searching for their camels and were instantly offered a cup of tea, as is customary in Bedouin culture. An elderly man in the family, seated in the middle, was leading the conversation about the rainy season that year, better grazing spots for camels, and the history of the coffee grinder or *misebeh* that he owned, which had been passed down from one generation to another.

Although they hold little power, tribal leaders are often singled out for their wisdom and leadership, based on consensus in the community. The community relies heavily on the leader's moral authority rather than the enforcement of law and order. His main function is that of an arbitrator. During the Arab Spring, however, a group of Jordanian tribal leaders and retired military officers criticized the government's domestic economic and political policies. They demanded privileges, services, and increased public sector employment as poverty and unemployment rates continued to climb, especially in rural areas.

Back in the tent, tea was served first, followed by the grinding ritual of coffee beans and cardamom, signalling that coffee would be served soon. When we returned to Ibraheem's home, he explained how much meeting for coffee is valued among Bedouins:

When the coffee is being served, everyone adjusts their seating position, to concentrate on the very act of pouring the coffee and taking the coffee cup. The focus must be on the person serving the coffee, so they know how valued they are, and on the coffee as well. You must always take the cup and hold it with your right hand. You must drink the first cup, taste it, and then the second and then the third. A Bedouin must have three cups only. If you're sitting with foreigners or strangers or people who are not from here, they would think badly of you if you drink more. Coffee is not like water, it's special and one must drink it consciously.

'What do you discuss over coffee?' I asked.

'I'll tell you exactly,' he answered.

'What is important to people here?' I interrupted. 'Do you talk about the news?'

The conversations go something like, 'Where are your camels today? I want to send my own to graze in such-and-such an area. What do you think?' They may say there are better spots, so they name places, and we know all the areas by heart. As for news, we just mention the headlines. We know generally what's going on of course, but we mostly talk about what matters to us: our children, our camels, our cattle. The animals are so precious to the Bedouins; they are essentially our livelihood.

Although camels are no longer the primary method of transport as they once were, they are often the main source of milk, hair, used for clothes and blankets, and a means for financial success. 'Thank God we have not had to sell any of our camels, because owning a camel is like owning gold—it is always in demand and provides financial security,' said Sultan.

At 7 a.m. the following day, a cold and slightly windy spring morning, Sultan was sent by his father to take their five camels to graze in the desert. The young man walked for hours, and led the camels with their front legs loosely bound by bright green rope so that they wouldn't stray too far. The spotted family dog named Qarnas, or 'hawk' in Arabic, walked beside him.

Four hours later, we drove for more than a quarter of an hour to find Sultan in the desert. He was sitting on a mountain top with no one and nothing around him except Qarnas. When Sultan saw the car, he pulled his long woollen *thobe*, an ankle-length one-piece cloak, around him for warmth and walked slowly to the pickup truck, his black slippers noticeably narrower and smaller than his feet. Instead of the traditional *kufiya*, he wore a red scarf, wrapped loosely around his head, held on by heavy coils or *agal*. Bedouins wear these to protect themselves from cold and wind, as well as to shield themselves from the sun and heat.

Sultan drove the pickup truck and was anxious to return home to drink and eat. He told me he had declined, out of shyness, an invitation for food and water by Bedouins who had spotted him and his camels. Qarnas ran behind the truck and returned home a few hours later. When Sultan was busy recovering from his trip that morning, I met with Sultan's sisters, Ahlam and Aseel, who were returning from school and running in and out of the house. They were anxious to show me the family's two rabbits, a new-born goat, and some olive trees. The two sisters told me that, unlike their father, Sultan seldom gets angry. When they were growing up, they had played games together, and he had studied with them. 'He is independent and wiser than his years,' they said, as they peeked into a wooden cage searching for the rabbits. 'Growing up, he was our brother, our friend, and like a father to us.' He was also stubborn, they admitted, and proud.

Although Sultan is traditional and conservative, he had a moment of rebellion when he was eighteen. He wanted to explore life outside of his village and Wadi Rum. He was tempted by the faster pace of life in Amman and other cities. At the time, he was also communicating online with a young woman who was at university in the capital. Without his father's knowledge, he rented a taxi, planning to stay and work in Amman. 'When I went there, I thought this is different, this is nice,' explained Sultan, as he sat in the guest area of his home surrounded by red and black mattresses. 'I met the girl, we went out to a café, but I explained to her I was not ready for marriage,' he recalled as he poured tea. Unlike his life in the village, he barely knew anyone in the city, and because of his anonymity he felt like he had fewer social obligations. He could be young there. However, he was unable to navigate the streets with the taxi he had rented, so he eventually returned home.

> You see fields, you see gardens. There's a lot of greenery compared to here, you see big markets, so many people, so many lights. You see a different life altogether. I'll tell you something though. I interacted with Jordanians in the city when I was training in the military and when I rented the taxi. Sometimes I wouldn't understand some of the words they were saying, and other times they didn't understand some words I was saying. They didn't know what a Bedouin's life is like. After a while, I came back. Perhaps this is the place where I am meant to be.

In the middle of his military training, he returned home for a break and decided he wanted to get married. He was considering marrying his cousin, Nisreen, a practice common among Bedouins, though they had hardly even spoken to each other.

> When I finished, I told my father and we went to visit them. I didn't love the girl and she didn't love me. I would be lying to you if I told you we loved each other. I thought it was better to choose someone I kind of knew than a stranger. So, what made me propose to her wasn't love or anything like that. I didn't need the love. What made me propose to her was that she was a respectable housewife who

would protect my honour. I know her behaviour generally, she's not silly like other girls nowadays. That's what made me choose her. Her family approved of me because they know I had established myself. I don't hang out with losers. I don't smoke.

When we first met, we didn't talk at all. I didn't ask her if she approved of me and she didn't ask if I approved of her. We only knew what the other looked like. I didn't know what she was like inside or what she thought about. At the engagement, we sat next to each other, and it was hard to interact. I wasn't used to her and she wasn't used to me. It's as if we hardly accepted each other.

It took three months from the engagement for me to convince her to let me hug her or kiss her. It took her two months to get to know who I really was. I also got to know her. I kept on trying to know what was on her mind, what she was thinking about, what she needs. We began discussing the future, what we were going to do. Our engagement lasted seven months and as soon as we felt we knew each other and were comfortable, we got married.

Sultan and Nisreen were married in September 2016, when he was twenty-one years old and she was only sixteen. On his days off, Sultan spends his time with Nisreen. They play cards, camp in the desert, or watch Arabic soap operas. Being close to the Saudi border, Sultan was influenced by music and television from the Arab Gulf states. Both Sultan and Nisreen prefer to spend their weekends camping under the open sky, lighting a fire, barbecuing, playing cards. But at night, Sultan lays out a blanket in his truck and they sleep there.

'Maybe there are scorpions, maybe there are snakes. Nisreen feels safer sleeping in the pickup when we camp,' he told me. It was something his grandparents would never have said or done as Bedouins who lived their entire lives in tents, as nomads.

Although Nisreen completed the basic ten-year compulsory education, Sultan does not want his wife to work or interact with other men in a work environment. Similar sentiments were not only expressed to me by those living in Manshieh but by a few other families across Jordan. At first, I asked Sultan what he would think if his wife were given the opportunity to work in an all-women environment, but he said it would be unacceptable to him. He did not want to come home and find his wife just coming back from work and tired. When I asked about her working part-time, he added that he did not like her going out and interacting with other people.

After Sultan returned from sending the camels to graze, I met Nisreen. She wore a tight black shirt with thin shoulder straps, her shiny black hair covering half her face, including the bright pink lipstick she wore. When she sat down next to Sultan, they held hands. They were giggling and smiling as if they had just met. She was four months pregnant at the time and spent her days watching dubbed Turkish and Gulf television series.

When Sultan is on duty all day and in the evening, Nisreen visits her mother-in-law, aunts, and other family members who live in Wadi Rum. The couple took me on a tour of their bright sparkling home. It was a sharp contrast from Nisreen's grandparents' life in the tent we had visited the day before. Sultan had designed the kitchen to overlook the television in their living room. In their kitchen, they had a washing machine, dishwasher, and a stove. 'Whenever I make money, I buy us more things for the house,' said Sultan.

There are several camel races every year in Wadi Rum, but the most famous take place at the Sheikh Zayed Heritage Festival, supervised by the Emirates Camel Racing Federation. More than ten years ago, the use of child jockeys in official camel races was prohibited by law in countries like Qatar and the United Arab Emirates. The jockeys have been replaced by robots, which consist of a receiver and body frame, a motor, and a whip that resembles a fishing rod without a handle or a hook. The robots are controlled by their trainers who communicate with the camel by walkie-talkie.

Sultan was only sixteen years old the first time he raced a camel. No one had taught him how to train his camels, so for several weeks he had observed how others were training theirs. Although the training is time consuming—it can take several months—camels are fast learners, and seldom forget what they are taught. Unlike horses, they are also known neither to forgive nor to forget any slights against them. If they are harmed, they exact revenge.

At the time, the family had three camels and Sultan chose to train two of them. For one month, he rode one and led the other with a halter. The camel he was training to race was the one with the halter, and as they trained together he learned how to steer her, how to make her sit and jog at a steady speed. He tried this with two of his camels and eventually chose Meran, the one who performed better and had more endurance. He trained her for one more month and then took her to the race track, where they practiced with the robot. In her first race, Meran ranked fourth out of nearly thirty-five camels. One month later, in her second race, she came in first. Between the two races, the family earned nearly $1,000. After Meran fell ill, Sultan stopped participating in camel races.

Meran was out grazing with the other camels. 'I'll show you the champion when we bring her back from the desert,' Sultan said. He would later admit female camels make better racers than male camels.

The following day, Ibraheem told us he planned to send Sultan to check on their camels in the desert. Sultan drove the pickup truck, patiently stopping every few minutes to look into the distance. Sometimes he relied on his eyesight; other times he used binoculars. We searched what seemed like half the desert for the camels. Sultan would later remark that calmness and patience were key to life in the desert.

There was no sign of the family's five camels. Whenever I pointed at a herd of camels in the distance, Sultan could immediately recognize that they were not his. After nearly three hours, the search was called off and we returned home. Ibraheem had prepared lunch—rice and red beans. Instead of serving the food onto dishes, he ate from the side of the tray with a spoon, as he called his younger children to join him. Years of experience backed Ibraheem's confidence that the camels would return home safely. 'They know there is water here,' he commented, as he poured hot, sweet tea after the meal. 'Remember, they don't forget.'

We returned home and watched the sheep and goat kid roam, encircled by a low fence and half-broken wood posts. Sultan quickly went inside and reappeared cradling his youngest sister in his arms, showing her the infant goat. Since becoming a soldier, Sultan has been unable to spend time with any of the family's animals other than the camels. His brother Mohammad has mainly taken on the role of tending to the flock's needs.

As Sultan spoke about his shift at the military school, he pointed to the dirt road and broke into a gleeful smile. Four of his camels had appeared, seemingly out of nowhere. They were walking together on the small road towards their home with Mohammad behind them in the distance. He was returning from school, wearing his school military uniform and carrying two books in his hands.

When the rest of the family saw the camels, they rushed outside. It felt almost like a celebration. Aseel and Ahlam ran back into the house and emerged with an aluminium bucket of water. In another bucket, Ibraheem and Sultan quickly poured wheat they had stored in a small room. The camels drank all the water and ate all the wheat. The family gathered around them. One of the camels was still standing in the middle of the dirt road; she would not drink, or eat, or follow orders. Sultan called her again and again, but she simply stood there. She stubbornly refused to move, until her calf appeared.

'Do you ever fear that this lifestyle—of being in nature, in the desert—and people's close ties with each other could disappear in the future?' I asked Sultan.

The desert, the way of life, will never disappear. The desert is as big as Jordan, it stretches all the way to the Saudi border. The desert belongs to no one, yet it is for everyone. Bedouins will always go there because no matter where they live or how they're forced to change, it's in their blood. They want to be surrounded by nature.

8

VIVA LA DIVA

SHIRENE RIFAI

She is a person who wants to be known for what she wears, but also judged by what she does. Part of her job is to wear one item or another: a watch, a necklace, a handbag. On some days, she models all three at the same time. As brand ambassador, she often represents and promotes products for companies.

The first time I met Shirene, she walked into the café of a five-star Amman hotel with a cup of coffee in one hand and a small Perrier in the other. Her long, stylish, highlighted hair was flowing and a green feathered vest covered her short skirt. In between sips of coffee, she pulled a thin cigarette from her purse and lit it. 'I can't think without my cigarette, and I hate it,' she said, inhaling deeply. 'At the same time, it makes me happy.' She exhaled, 'Does that make sense?'

Three months after our first meeting, the lawyer turned fashionista announced that after fifteen years of smoking, she was quitting. 'To become stronger than a cigarette! I decided to regain control over my life [and] to quit that filthy habit,' she posted to her 80,000 social media followers. A few days later, she shared a live video on Instagram encouraging her followers who smoke to kick the habit.

Shirene rarely smiles and her demeanour—serious, confident, proud—can be intimidating. She stands out, attracts attention, and can at times seem standoffish. In reality, she is quite affable. She often replies to queries she receives online and regularly mentors upcoming designers and social media enthusiasts. Her guidance is her way of giving back to the community. She is not only a brand ambassador but an influencer too.

During a speaker series called 'How Jordan is innovative in Fashion Design', Shirene offered her advice to a crowd of young and upcoming artists, bloggers, and designers. 'It's not enough to have panels and just talk,' Shirene told me after the event. 'We need to support young fashion designers. We need to create a fashion fund. We lack everything.'

She is demanding at work; she instructs photographers during photo shoots and often lectures clients. It is part of her success as a creative: a luxury consultant, brand manager, and social media influencer—businesses that are constantly evolving.

Shirene describes herself as 'roaming the world, searching for everything fashion … Known for her first-row appearances at Paris Fashion Week.' From her photos to her clothing style, she could be a glamorous model from anywhere, London or Los Angeles. Her life presents a striking contrast to the impressions of Jordan as a conservative society.

As in other countries, a small but influential elite exists in Jordan, mainly in West Amman. Notably, they come from influential political or business families. Shirene's husband, Mohammed Rifai, has two former prime ministers in his family: an uncle and a cousin.

West Amman began booming in the eighties, and with that boom, class divisions were fuelled. West Amman has been taking the lion's share of the country's infrastructure development and investment, with upscale hotels being built, covered in glass or shining white stone. Amman's west side is the scene of its more lively nightlife, boasting a selection of upscale restaurants serving international cuisine—Asian, Italian, and French.

East Amman is crowded and underdeveloped; West Amman is appealing and trendy. Homes in the west are covered in thick white limestone, while many buildings in the east are built with slabs of beige concrete. 'The inhabitants of the western part feel that they are strangers in the eastern part, while the inhabitants of the eastern part feel like pariahs in the west,' Mohammad Fdilat wrote of Amman in *As-Safir Arabi*, an Arab daily political newspaper.

This social divide remains a challenge and contributes to the perception of corruption that was the biggest complaint among Jordanians during the Arab Spring protests. Initially, the Arab Spring inspired calls for reform, including revisions to the Jordanian constitution and changes in the electoral laws, but primarily demanded measures to combat corruption, a fight that continues today. In an article in *Foreign Policy*, Curtis Ryan, author of *Jordan and the Arab Uprisings*, wrote that while heightened tension and occasional violence in Jordan can partly be attributed to identity politics, these phenomena have, in fact, more to do with economics. 'While political tensions in Jordan frequently manifest in ethnic, tribal, or identity terms,' Ryan wrote, 'they are often more deeply about class divisions between rich and poor, and between haves and have-nots. And these cut across ethnic lines.'

Amman acts as the country's economic hub. One of the relatively new projects to emerge is a 'new' downtown called Abdali. The large complex hosts a lavish mall filled with brand-name stores and cafés, a boulevard, hotels, retail outlets and residential towers. When Shirene showed me her pictures from a photo shoot at Abdali mall, I discussed this economic, social and cultural schism with her, and how some Jordanians might perceive her life and work as unconventional. She replied:

> I would say yes, I live in my own bubble, but even in my own bubble I'm trying to put Jordan on the map regarding fashion and exposure to the world, which I feel I am doing. When I travel, I am representing Jordan. You know everyone has a role to play and everyone is different. I can inspire, I can help even if I'm in this bubble. I also like politics—my husband's family is into politics, so I know what's going on. But that's me. That's me but it does not mean I don't know what's happening in my country, that I don't know there are challenges.

When Shirene was growing up, both her parents worked full-time. Her father, Mazen, was a lawyer; her mother, Nehaya, was an English teacher who then became a public relations manager at an airline company. 'After I got married,' recalled Shirene, 'my parents told me not to become a housewife.'

She has an image of her father sitting late at night working on his cases. Her fashion-conscious mother was dedicated to her job, working long hours on lesson plans and marking papers. In the late sixties and early seventies, her father was still an intern at a law firm. Nehaya, who was a teacher at the time, was the main breadwinner in the family until Mazen completed his training and education.

'She gave birth to me,' Shirene said, 'and a week later she took me with her to school and had the students regularly check on me. She had another side as well—she loved life, even now. She would be ill and getting ready to go to the doctor, and she would still dress up.'

Shirene remembers a childhood similar to other Jordanians who grew up in the seventies and eighties in West Amman. Then, the capital was less urban—emptier plots of land, more trees and fewer people. Weekends were spent at her grandparents' home, and after-school hours were whiled away outdoors playing with neighbours and cousins in the streets—hide and seek, hot and cold—until dusk.

She lives in the area she grew up in, Um Uthaina, a tranquil, classy neighbourhood that has become more crowded in the past decade as more residents—humanitarian aid offices, wealthy Iraqis fleeing the wars, foreign diplomats—continue to move in. When she was growing up, the main market there included a vegetable stall with boxes of fruit and vegetables displayed along the front. There was a small stationery shop next door, with an old worn-out table covered with lined notebooks, coloured pens and pencils, and small firecrackers. Across the street stood a supermarket that sold imported chocolates. The market has now been converted into a row of upscale jewellery shops, including the luxury brand Chopard, which Shirene has promoted as a social media influencer.

Throughout her life, Shirene attended private schools in Amman and scored well in her general secondary examination or *Tawjihi*. She liked dressing up and styling her hair even when she was at school. She often used to travel with her family on holiday. Sometimes her parents travelled on their own, and her mother would return home with bags full of fashionable clothes for her children. As a teenager, Shirene would be excited about her new outfits, so much so that she would wake up early to wear them to school the next day.

Shirene went on to study law at the University of Jordan, a public institution. Her father had picked her up from university nearly every day, and she had hoped to follow in his footsteps. 'It was a shock,' she recalled, remembering university. 'It was extremely tough but I enjoyed the challenge.' Her shock had arisen during her first exam, when she noticed that many of the students in her class were cheating.

During her free time, she used to go to a popular social club, equipped with swimming pools, a bowling alley, and tennis courts. One day, during her third year at university, Shirene went to the club with her friends to watch a tennis match. A young man about her age named Mohammed was also there and noticed her. When they met later at a party, he asked her friends about her. A few days later, Shirene decided to take a break from studying and went to the social club on her own. As she entered, she saw Mohammed leaving. 'I blocked him out,' she said, with a half-smile. 'He was not my type. I liked bad boys and he was calm, cool and collected.' Mohammed, who had just finished a tennis match, asked if he could join her. 'We sat there, we talked, we clicked. He took my mind off everything and I remember we just spent hours talking.'

A short time later, he sent her a message telling her he would be in the southern port of Aqaba for Eid Al-Fitr, a holiday marking the end of Ramadan, and that he had a boat. Her family would be going as well. The pair met in Aqaba. She spent the day with him on the boat, along with mutual friends and her brother, Abdullah. As soon as they returned to Amman, Mohammed asked Shirene out and she accepted.

> After being together for a year, I figured that I was in love with him. We were sitting on a swing and suddenly there were tears in my eyes. He said, 'What's the matter?' I was like, 'I love you,' just like that out of the blue. And he was like, 'Me too.' But we were very young. I never thought about getting married. My friends were thinking about it the whole time, but I never did.

Mohammed proposed to her after she graduated. She scrapped plans to go to Europe to continue studying when she saw two of her friends, a couple, split up because one of them wanted to study abroad and the other didn't. Shirene was afraid her plans would end her relationship with Mohammed. She didn't want to lose him.

On 7 September 1995, Mohammed and Shirene were married. A year into their marriage, she was already turning into a housewife. She would spend her days visiting her mother or her friends, 'but we were all bored and we felt useless.' A year later, her parents told her to find work. She began volunteering at INJAZ, a non-profit organization that aims to bridge gaps between the education system and the needs of the labour market.

Meanwhile, Shirene's 'bubble' was expanding. In fact, it had been growing ever since university. The students there came from all across the nation and from many different political and socioeconomic backgrounds. There were even times, she said, that she felt out of place there. As a volunteer at INJAZ, she mentored female students who were less privileged and who had attended public schools.

Throughout that time, her friends would turn to her for fashion advice. She would mix and match clothes for them. She still revamps their wardrobes. She enjoyed this role so much that she turned it into a career in fashion. After she completed her volunteer work at INJAZ, she was hired as a fashion editor by a local English-language lifestyle magazine.

As soon as she was hired, her editors suggested she manage a photo shoot. The first shoot she organised was inspired by Audrey Hepburn, the iconic film star renowned for her elegance. It took Shirene three weeks to prepare, to convince shops at a mall in Amman to open for her, to describe to them what a photo shoot would look like, to come up with the hair and makeup concepts, to contact the model and locations.

> We were shooting at this restaurant that just opened, there were customers there and some of them looked at us like what we were doing was a scandal, like what the hell was I doing with a model in a restaurant like that? We shot part of it in the Dead Sea as well. It was a great experience, but it was also insane.

Shirene's passion for media and fashion deepened. She worked with a photographer, supervised photo shoots and a three-page spread in the magazine, and also began administering content, attracting sponsorship, and planning for awards ceremonies.

Her editors then asked her to manage a new magazine specializing in weddings. Every issue was a new project. She came up with ideas, produced content, hired photographers, and managed photo shoots, but also generated advertising. A month and a half later, she was visiting her mother-in-law, who upon seeing her burst into tears. 'She asked me, "Why do you look like this? You've lost so much weight." I was stressed. It killed me. I did everything on my own.'

Her days were busy and her nights long. She was also raising her two sons, Kareem and Rakan. 'I wasn't a bad mum and wife, but work was definitely a priority in my life.' For the most part, she managed to balance her work for the magazine with family life, and was there to help her sons with their homework after school. Yet there were times when she would constantly be on the phone, even at home. 'Most of the time, I would leave work, do homework with them, and return to the office,' she recalled.

> It was hard, but I was happy. I was happy at work and I was happy at home. It was not easy but I had support. Before I took on the job, I told my husband, 'If you're not going to be like a wall I can lean on, to be my support, then I cannot do it.' I asked him, 'Shall I go for it?' He told me, 'Yes, go for it.' Now of course there were times when he would say I was crazy, I was doing too much, but it worked out because my husband was wonderful, is still wonderful, my boys are flourishing amazingly, and I still have my girlfriends. I have a social life. I got it back, especially now after some time has passed.

Eventually, Shirene became editor-in-chief of another lifestyle and fashion magazine. She even launched a men's lifestyle magazine. After several years, management decided to decrease the number of pages, the budget was reduced, and they began laying off staff. Shirene said she felt the quality would be impacted, so she eventually left as well.

VIVA LA DIVA: SHIRENE RIFAI

In early 2000, there was a boom in the number of Arabic- and English-language cultural and lifestyle magazines published in Jordan, but very few are still operating today. Many were forced to shut down with the advent of digitization and the rapid switchover from print to online, as well as because of shrinking budgets. Mainly though, there was a proliferation in the market of bad management, weak content, and lack of long-term strategic plans.

> Today, as a consultant, I go to the companies, I tell them, 'I don't come in with you just to snap photos and to look like this or that.' Most of the time I make an actual plan for them. What I'm saying, it's about Jordan. The country has a lot to offer but nobody to direct this field. One of the important things—and by the way, social media is so important for Jordan—is having people who know how to lead.

When I met Shirene for the first time in early 2017, she told me about a photo shoot she was doing to celebrate Mother's Day. She asked if I wanted to attend and sent me a map to her friend's house. When I arrived at the upscale home, filled with avant-garde art and with a well-kept garden, I found Shirene and her two friends deep in conversation with a photographer, a videographer, and a marketing team representing the jewellery brands she was showcasing.

Shirene met her two friends eighteen years ago at the social club when their children were still in pushchairs. Now they were all being models for Mother's Day. Lina is a forty-five-year-old dentist; Nadine is forty-two and co-owns a copyright and translation house. Shirene was in charge that day, directing the photographer, the videographer, and her friends. The three women were goofing around, posing, giggling, gossiping. It was a side of Shirene I had not seen before.

'Act natural, we want to show the earrings,' the photographer told the three women. 'Don't move, you're not being not natural.'

Lina and Nadine confessed to me later, nothing they did that day came naturally to them. Modelling was something they had never done before. 'Any luck?' they asked the photographer. 'Are we there? Are we getting there?'

They fixed the jewellery they were wearing—gold double bracelets, large hoop earrings, rings with flashy stones. 'Is this posing natural?' asked Lina.

'We found it,' the women all said in unison.

'Can you move your hair at the same time, so all the earrings can show?' the photographer told them as they posed again in the garden area.

'We didn't realize how difficult fashion is,' Lina told me later, drinking coffee.

Hours passed, and as Shirene was changing dresses upstairs, I asked the brand manager assistant for Chopard in Jordan why they had chosen Shirene as an influencer. She had also been appointed as the brand ambassador for TRESemmé, Unilever's premium hair care brand, and Tufenkjian Jewelry. The marketing manager told me they were tapping into her influential social media profile and that his team was focusing on Instagram to promote their brand and products. 'Shirene is part of where we need to go.'

Lina and Nadine came down wearing white knee-length dresses. Shirene wore light brown open-toe lace-up boots and a matching dress embroidered with fuchsia flowers, a silver design, and a yellow leaf.

Her secret is research, and speaking in the brand's tone of voice when showcasing its products. 'But what is more important than that is when one way or another you actually give back to the community and this is what I would like to do. When you are a brand ambassador you can empower. You should be able to empower.' She posted a live video about how she felt during the first week after she quit smoking: sleepless nights, racing thoughts, headaches. It is not easy, she said on camera, but you can quit too. She is also aware of how the Middle East region is seen in the West—war, oppression, extremism—so she shares videos and photos to show another side to the region.

A few weeks later, on a cold evening, I visited Shirene at home. It was getting dark and she greeted me outside, having just arrived from an appointment. She lives on a quiet street with her husband and her son Kareem. Their other son, Rakan, is studying electrical engineering in the United Kingdom and so is away for most of the year.

The entrance to the home overlooks a public school sheltered by a concrete wall. Shireen has been living in the same house for twenty-two years, and it sits just two streets down from the home she grew up in. Through the front door was an exercise machine. The room was dim, lit only by candles. The living room area had glass and wooden vases and statues; family photos and oriental paintings hung on the wall.

She poured Turkish coffee for us in small blue and white ceramic cups. She had prepared a plate full of desserts, chocolate éclairs and different coloured macarons. Shirene described her husband as a 'hardcore banker' and said they led different lives. He is organized, and she is 'all over the place'.

Shirene was preparing to travel to Rome for three days. A wedding and evening wear company had invited her to an annual fashion show. She was showcasing an evening dress by them as well. She held her two mobile phones, as always, with an extended battery charger and a white cord trailing behind. When I asked her later what she was doing with her phone, she answered 'snapping'—or using the social media app Snapchat. She wanted to post part of our meeting to Instagram as a silent live video as well.

Her son Kareem joined us. He described himself as more like his father than his mother, but serious like Shirene. He had helped her to take off on Instagram by taking a picture of her that she had used as her first post. She had received many responses, and so he encouraged her to continue. Since then, StyleArabia.com has named her as one the Top 20 Best Instagram Fashion Accounts to follow in the Middle East.

When I asked Kareem what he thinks of his mum, he described her as confident, strong, and someone who 'goes after what she wants'. He remembered his mother working all his life, and added that their only time to bond these days was after midnight, when they watched American television series. Otherwise, he said, he was too busy studying, while she was too busy with work and managing things at home.

It was already dark when we walked outside. Shireen described some of the outdoor renovations they had had done over the past years. I asked her if she was happy with where she was in life now.

I'm happy but I want more. I still want more. Now I can do more … Very few people know what I'm going to tell you. I feel that fashion continues to be underestimated, people think that fashion is silly. Fashion isn't silly. You cannot get up in the morning without looking good. It took me some time to make people understand that fashion is in everything. You want to sell, you must look good. If you want to be a good wife, you need to look good. Fashion is in everything. So, I'm continuously showing the outside world that we are more than what they see, and inside Jordan I'm showing them that fashion is important.

9

BETWIXT AND BETWEEN

JAMAL SHULTAF

For twenty-two years, he had waited to come to America. He remembers the exact date he landed in Chicago: Sunday, 12 February 2012. He felt disorientated by the piercing wind, the ways, the words.

At the age of forty, Jamal left behind everything he had ever known, not knowing when, or if, he would ever return. He abruptly quit his job as director of food and beverages at a renowned hotel chain on the Dead Sea, south of the capital. His wife and three children remained in their crowded neighbourhood in Amman until he had settled and found work.

'One keeps thinking there is hope in America,' reflected Jamal, who had his United States citizenship interview only one day before we met. 'Hope cannot be defined, but it's a powerful feeling that sustained me for so many years while I waited to come here.'

At first, he shared a small apartment with his brother, who worked as a chef in a restaurant all day. Arriving with only $200 in his pocket, there was little for him to do except watch everyone around him get on with their busy lives. 'The first forty days were extremely hard,' recalled Jamal, who has thick black hair, wide shoulders, and small dark eyes. He now lives in the work-ing-class southwestern suburb Chicago Ridge, Illinois. His apartment has thin walls and a small balcony overlooking a quiet road paved with giant trees, with lush green grass beneath.

'I couldn't find any work. No one has any time for you here. I felt lost. I was in a country where I felt like I didn't know any-one.' There were days when he would call his wife, Faten, and tell her that he was contemplating giving it all up and returning to Jordan.

'I encouraged him to stay,' Faten told me when I visited her at home. 'We worked too hard to reach this point. God is generous. I told him not to depend on anyone except himself. If you depend on people, you won't get anywhere.'

Jamal decided to persevere. He heeded his wife's advice. He borrowed a car from his brother and went to different restaurants to ask if they would hire him. Given the slower workload during the winter months and his limited English skills, managers weren't willing to hire him. Then he began going to work with his brother. Jamal watched him cook, fry, and grill. He wanted to see how people interacted with each other.

According to the Arab American Institute Foundation, there are nearly 3.7 million Arabs living in the United States. In past decades, their numbers have grown exponentially as conflicts and economic crises continue to plague the Middle East. The first wave of Jordanians migrated to the United States in the late fifties, nearly ten years after Jordan secured its independence from Great Britain. They emigrated from Jordan as a result of the First Arab–Israeli War, according to the Encyclopedia of Chicago.

At the time, Jordan was still in control of the West Bank, and so Jordanians from the East Bank and Palestinians from the West Bank both travelled with Jordanian passports, 'creating the undefined category "Palestinian-Jordanian".' The new immigrants, who were mainly Jordanian Christians—specifically Eastern Orthodox Christians—settled near the west side of Chicago, which includes Greektown and Little Italy, and the southwest side, which includes a mix of affluent, working-class, and poor communities. The Greater Chicago area is home to one of the largest Palestinian communities in America as well as to Lebanese, Syrians, and Assyrians, one of the oldest Christian ethnic groups who trace their origins to today's Middle East.

According to data released by the Chicago Police Department, 2016 was the deadliest year in nearly two decades with more than 4,000 shooting victims. Still, as the third largest city in the United States, it remains a main economic hub nationwide and is known for its innovative architecture and businessmen who rebuilt Chicago after the great fire of 1871. The Willis Tower, better known as Sears Tower, was the tallest building in the world for twenty-five years. O'Hare International Airport, where Jamal landed, is one of the busiest airports in the world, recording a total of 78 million passengers in 2016.

Before he came to Chicago Ridge, Jamal lived in a small apartment in a working-class neighbourhood in East Amman with his parents, wife, and three children. He spent his days working by the Dead Sea, around 40 minutes away from Amman by car. As a waiter in the hotel industry, he depended on the flow of tourists for work. Although his monthly salary steadily increased to reach almost $800 at his last job, he was still living hand to mouth. He bought essential groceries, paid the bills and covered his university tuition.

Both of Jamal's parents came to Jordan from Palestine during the Arab–Israeli War of 1948 and settled in the Al-Korah district in the northern town of Irbid, close to the Syrian border. Jamal was born there, but his family moved to Zarqa, a gritty, working-class city northeast of Amman, a year later. His father, a civil servant, was transferred to the Department of Land and Survey, an administration that mainly deals with land ownership and property rights.

Jamal grew up with his parents and eight siblings, all crammed together into a two-bedroom apartment. He and his brothers stayed in one room, their parents in the other. His three sisters slept in the living room. The family of eleven shared one bathroom, and because there was no shower, they had to fill buckets with water, heat it, add soap and wash themselves. 'I'm not going to lie,' said Jamal. 'No one in my family was happy, especially my mother, who wanted to move from that place, badly.'

Jamal attended one of the UN Relief and Works Agency (UNRWA) schools set up for Palestinian refugees after the Arab–Israeli wars. Back then, the UN schools were known for their high-quality basic and continuing education. When he was twelve years old, his family moved into a more spacious apartment in a less crowded area called Wadi Al-Hajar, or 'stone valley'. As Jamal and his siblings grew up, the youngest helped their parents around the home while the older ones began to work. In 1978, Jamal's brother, Abed, moved to Detroit in Michigan to study. Nearly four years after Abed landed there, he got married and had a son. The boy was born with American citizenship, and Abed's American wife later passed on her citizenship to her husband too.

Meanwhile, Jamal moved from the UN refugee school to a Jordanian public school. Like his older brother, who later became a doctor, he enjoyed science classes, including chemistry and biology. He knew he wanted to enter the scientific stream, but when he graduated he felt lost. 'The problem that young men faced back then, and maybe today as well, is the lack of career counselling,' said Jamal.

> Who was going to guide me? No one from school did. I was going down a path and suddenly I had nothing to do. Thank God, I had my brother, Mohammad, who told me to go to nursing school, but

I wasn't interested in nursing. I wanted to work in a medical lab but when I applied to a college in Russeifeh, they didn't accept me. I applied to another college in Zarqa and was accepted. My idea was to go there for two years, graduate and go to America.

Around the same time, Jamal's mother left for the United States to join Abed, who by then had filed petitions for his other siblings in Jordan to become lawful permanent residents. The process is not only lengthy but comprises many requirements, such as financial sponsorship, lengthy interviews, and background checks. The family knew it could take several years, and it was then that Jamal began imagining his life in America.

I would tell my friends, 'I'm going to America.' The idea was ingrained in me ever since high school. I knew I was going to leave. When my brother told my mother to join him, she was happy. We were all young men and she was worried about us and our future, she wanted to bring us all there.

Growing up in Zarqa spurred them on to seek a different life. Jamal watched his siblings graduate from college but remain unemployed. All his siblings used to think life was better and easier in America, even though they had never been there and had no certain employment prospects if they landed there. The perception of America, of what possibilities lay therein, was in many ways an escape from the life they were living.

One after another, Jamal's siblings packed their bags and left, but his own forms never arrived. His mother eventually decided to reapply on his behalf, but the process was delayed by several years when she left the United States to visit Jordan. As a result, her own permanent residency was cancelled and had to be reinstated before she could file Jamal's new application.

In the meantime, Jamal graduated from college as a lab technician. He not only enjoyed it but excelled at it, and said he had finally found his passion. Still, when he approached several private sector labs, he was turned away again and again, either because there were more qualified candidates with work experience or because of a lack of job openings.

> I searched and searched. I think I spent six months searching for a job, maybe more. I couldn't find any. Then I went to a lab close to our home and there was an old lady there. I told her I was looking for a job. She looked at me and said, 'We don't have any jobs for fresh graduates. We need someone with experience.'

Since the civil service is one of the main sources of employment for Jordanians, Jamal's relatives, including his father, advised him to apply to work in that sector until a position opened up in a private lab. Jamal was unconvinced. It would take years of waiting, he explained, and the entry salary was less than $300 a month. Even though public service employment is ostensibly regulated by open recruitment for positions, and selection is purportedly based on technical skills and availability of jobs, many Jordanians claim that favouritism and nepotism, collectively known as *wasta*, remain widely used. Jamal never applied.

In 1993, he gave up on his field of study and instead used his own connections to find a job. His uncle and brother were chefs at a high-end restaurant in Amman and Jamal informed them that he was desperate to find work. 'I told them, "Just try me out and I will learn." I was willing to do anything. I worked in the back, polishing silverware, preparing tea and coffee.' Jamal gradually worked his way up from back of house to become a busboy. Nearly a year later, he had the opportunity to work as a waiter and was eventually promoted to be an event organizer for upscale wedding parties at an international hotel chain nearby.

> I began seeing the world of parties. It was a different life, a different world. I was in a fantasy world. I didn't know an elite society existed in Jordan. Sometimes the other waiters and I would stand in the middle of the hall and just stare at guests. The music, the parties,

the clients, what they wore, what their life was like. They would sit together, dance with each other. I thought, what kind of life am I living? I was a resident of Zarqa.

In 2001, Jamal's mother became an American citizen. However, with no sign of his own paperwork for residency, Jamal opened a food stall with a friend in front of a university campus. It never took off and Jamal lost most of his savings. He was out of a job, and spent his days at a gym in Zarqa and hanging out with his friends. The 11 September 2001 attacks on the United States took their toll on the tourism industry in Jordan. Whenever Jamal went to apply for a job at a hotel, he would find, to his dismay, that far from hiring new employees, they were in fact making staff redundant.

The only job he found was at a hotel in Aqaba, the southern Jordanian port city on the Red Sea gulf. Jamal was employed in the food and beverage department and was assigned to the main restaurant. Three months later, the hotel laid off most of its staff. 'September 11 hit tourism so, so bad,' recalled Jamal. 'The manager told me, "As you can see, all the reservations have been cancelled. There isn't any work for you to do here."'

Mohammad, Jamal's brother and the doctor in the family, was visiting Jordan from Saudi Arabia. He wanted to help his two remaining brothers in Jordan, including Kamal, who was also unemployed. Mohammad rented a small restaurant in a working class, industrial area of Aqaba for his brothers to manage, specializing in falafel sandwiches, fava beans, and hummus. When, six months later, Kamal's US residency arrived, it was time for him to join the rest of the family in Chicago. Jamal remained in Aqaba, spending his evenings by the Red Sea, gazing at the glass-bottomed boats sailing across the water and wondering if, ever, his turn to leave would come.

'My family in Chicago said my paperwork was on its way to being approved and that I needed to be patient,' Jamal told me.

'I didn't know whether to get married in Jordan and build a future, whether I was going to continue working in hotels, or whether I was ever going to go to America.'

At thirty years old, he stayed in the hotel industry but moved to the Dead Sea as new hotels began springing up. He worked there for ten years, but he never gave up on his dream to leave. 'For so many years, I put my life on hold,' he said, when we met at a Dunkin' Donuts café near his apartment in Chicago. 'I was just waiting, so I knew I had to move on with my life as well.' His destiny, he thought at the time, was to remain in the hotel industry and to get married.

> Many young men like me thought we were stuck. That we wouldn't ever leave the country, so we might as well make do. In 2005, when I was thirty-three, I found my wife. I always thought that if I ever got married, I would be introduced to my future wife through one of my friends. So, this young work colleague called Shadi, may God bless him, called me after I told him I was looking for a wife and he said, 'My mother is telling you that my sister is available and you're a decent man, bring your mother and come see her.' So I made an appointment. I remember it was a Wednesday. As soon as I saw her, I agreed right away. I had seen other girls before but I felt I didn't click with any of them. With Faten, I felt it was our destiny to be together. When you meet a woman and you feel comfortable with her, it's destiny. So that day, I remember fate joined us together. When she also accepted me, we began having long conversations but the first thing I told her was that one day, I might go to America. She said, 'I will follow you, it's no problem.'

After Jamal's mother saw her sons succeed in America, she returned to Amman to be with her husband and her son. The siblings had some savings from their work in America and used it to buy a plot of land in Amman. They built an apartment building, giving one of the apartments to their parents. Jamal lived in it until he moved to Chicago.

BETWIXT AND BETWEEN: JAMAL SHULTAF

At thirty-three, Jamal felt he finally had a stable life. He was promoted at work, got married, and continued his education at a university in Zarqa. He wanted to earn a bachelor's degree and work as a medical lab scientist. He paid for the tuition from his salary and hoped one day to leave the hotel industry and pursue his new profession.

Between work and university, Jamal was always on the go. He would catch the first morning bus to work by the Dead Sea and, if he had classes that day, would not return home until 1 a.m. Faten would often be left alone with his parents, especially on weekdays. When his wife became pregnant a year later, Jamal finally received the news he had so waited for.

> My brother called me from Chicago, he said, 'Your paperwork arrived but when you applied, you were single. Now you're married and I heard that your wife is pregnant. Are you going to come here alone because that is what we applied for? Are you going to leave her behind in Jordan, or shall I submit another application on your behalf for both of you to come together? It means starting over again. It could take two, four, six years until you get the approval.' I told him, 'No problem.' I had waited already for a long time. 'I can't just go and leave my wife here and start from scratch. It would be unfair to her.' So I wasn't selfish, even though I had heard of others who had travelled and left their families behind.

While he waited, Jamal graduated from university. The couple had three children, Ammar, Hala, and Mohammad. Their father became a supervisor at the hotel chain. Through a bank loan, Jamal and his cousin opened a small café at a main market near the family's apartment in Amman.

> We were just starting out. Customers at the café could smoke hookah, play cards, and watch football matches. My cousin oversaw it and I stayed at my job in the hotel. It was then that my American approval forms arrived. I was so happy but also thought, oh God, I have no luck in starting anything.

Jamal and his family were called in for an interview at the US embassy in Amman. He underwent a medical check-up and filled out countless forms. Then, in 2010, the Arab Spring erupted. The process was delayed for another two years, during which time his first sponsor was rejected and Jamal was forced to find another. Finally, in January 2012, six years after his application was filed, he was granted residency. Two weeks later, Jamal left Jordan.

> I was scared. I had waited for this moment for so long but when the day came, I also realized that after twenty-two years of work in Jordan, I had to build a future from scratch. Reality set in. I was coming to a different world from the one I had imagined but knew nothing about. My brothers were there to help, yes, that's correct, but they also said that with my experience in the hotel industry, I wouldn't have a hard time finding a job here. That was not true, of course. I dreaded it. I thought, what if I don't make it here?

Today, the forty-five-year-old has built his new life in Chicago Ridge with reminders of Jordan everywhere. He works at a Middle Eastern restaurant and lives in a building surrounded by Arabic sounds. When he is online, he chats with his old friends and follows Al-Wehdat, a football club in Jordan.

His wife shops at the giant Walmart store but still cooks meals that remind her of their former home: aubergines, cauliflower with rice and meat, jute leaves or *molikyeh* with rice. Faten understands English but has yet to learn to speak it. Two years after she moved to America, she registered to attend English classes at a college. Jamal hired a tutor for her, but she continues to find the language difficult.

Jamal and Faten's three children attend public school and speak both English and Arabic fluently. They love playing video games. They have cereal for breakfast but for lunch prefer to eat luncheon meat sandwiches with Jordanian homemade *labneh*, or thick and creamy yoghurt spread, rather than the chicken nuggets and hot dogs served at their school.

BETWIXT AND BETWEEN: JAMAL SHULTAF

Hala and Mohammad were too young when they moved to remember anything about Jordan. Ammar, who came to America when he was seven, remembers spending time with his cousins in Amman, being close to his grandparents, and walking to a supermarket near their home. As is typical of first-generation Americans, because of Ammar's strong command of English and as the oldest sibling, he sometimes plays the role of language and culture mediator between his parents and other Americans.

Since he arrived in his new home, Jamal has sought to strike a balance between what is practical, what is possible, and what may not be. After he realized his limited language skills would hold him back from most jobs, he decided to seek employment at Middle Eastern restaurants. He researched what cafés and restaurants were available and visited each one.

Not far from his home, in the southwest suburb of Bridgeview, there is a popular restaurant called Al Bawadi Grill. It serves kebabs, hummus, and a wide range of Arabic soups and salads. It also cultivates a Middle Eastern atmosphere with lanterns, plastic camels, fake palm trees, and recreated scenes from the Badia region, of traditional Arab homes in the semi-arid desert of Syria and Jordan. Servers come around with piping hot coffee in a *dalleh*, or coffee pot, wearing red *kufiyas* or headdresses, beige *thobes*, and brown leather strappings across their chest and waist, traditionally worn by desert-roaming Bedouins to store bullets and knives. When I spoke with the owner, Khalil Ismail, he told me that he wanted to reconstruct scenes from a home he had left behind more than thirty years ago.

The restaurant's tinted windows, its ambiance, and the mainly Arab-American customers can make it easy to forget that one is not in fact in the Middle East. On Memorial Day, a federal holiday for remembering people who died while serving in the United States Armed Forces, the restaurant was full. Customers from diverse backgrounds—Caucasians, Asians, African-Americans, and Hispanics—waited up to half an hour for an empty table. I visited Jamal at work that day, but he was busy taking orders and bringing plates piled high with food from the kitchen. That day, I just watched him work and we barely spoke.

The first two times that Jamal had applied to work there, he had been turned away. The third time he visited Al Bawadi, he found a former colleague from Jordan who was employed there. Jamal shared how desperate he was to work, requesting to speak to the management, who finally agreed to hire him. He began working there part-time.

The restaurant environment provided Jamal with a sense of comfort and familiarity. It was there at Al Bawadi that I first met him. Like all the waiters there, he was wearing a traditional Syrian uniform: a white and black *kufiya* wrapped around his head like a bandana, a loose thick black shirt, baggy black trousers, and a white *kufiya* wrapped around his waist. I asked him if he was from Jordan and if he liked his life in America so far. 'My life here improved quickly,' he answered in a low voice as he held a notepad to take orders. 'My children are receiving a type of education I would not be able to afford to give them in Jordan. Even if I was here solely for their future, it's worth it.'

When Jamal wasn't working at the restaurant, he was driving a truck, delivering dessert packages to shops. From his second job, he learned his way around, discovering places and roads that once seemed alien. Sometimes he made more money in two days than he used to in a month in Jordan. He bought furniture, games for his children, and a silver SUV that he proudly showed me as we were leaving Dunkin' Donuts.

Faten's first words when I met her were, 'I miss Jordan. I wish I could go back and smell the earth after it rains there.' Their apartment is on the third and last floor of a building with a tight and dark staircase. Near the family's apartment door, a small, round, misty window was half open, the view outside obscured by bright green leaves. The only light in the building came from the shining spaces between tree branches. Inside the apartment, a wide television had been taken over by the children's video games.

Faten is petite with thick wide eyebrows, the sides of which are partially hidden by the colourful hijabs she wears. When I asked her what she thought of America when she first arrived, she grew silent as she recollected her first impressions.

> I thought the doors, the windows, and the balconies were smaller than in Jordan. I thought, why do all the houses look the same? I felt some of the Arabs here were nosey, but later I thought life is nicer here. Americans in particular mind their own business. One has freedom. Even my husband and me, the nature of our relationship together has totally changed. We have our privacy.

At the beginning, Faten, like Jamal, had a hard time adapting to her new home. For two years after she arrived, Faten was too afraid to leave the apartment. Jamal, working two jobs, was away most of the day. The three children were attending school. Jamal kept insisting, or as Faten called it, 'nagging', that she learn how to drive, make new friends and explore their neighbourhood. Instead she remained at home, cleaning, preparing meals, and sometimes just pacing back and forth. Jamal had hoped that having Arab neighbours would bring his family comfort and a sense of familiarity but the couple quickly realized they were not in Jordan anymore. No one had time to socialize, and their neighbours tended to keep to themselves.

> When I learned how to drive, my whole life changed. Before that I was depressed. I began buying groceries on my own, taking my kids to the doctors. I no longer had to wait for Jamal's day off to do everything. In fact, I began dropping him off at work sometimes. Life here requires patience. If you aren't patient and don't endure the hardships at the beginning, you will not make it.

On January 27, 2017, shortly after becoming president, Donald Trump issued an executive order suspending entry to the United States from seven Middle Eastern and African countries. Despite the protests and legal challenges, including a nationwide temporary restraining order, and even though Jordan was not on the list, Jamal felt fearful. The family had booked tickets to go home to visit their families after a five-year absence, but Jamal quickly cancelled the trip.

> Although [the ban] was overturned, I still wanted to guarantee we could return. People were afraid to travel and of being unable to enter again, even people with passports or residency cards. It was all so unpredictable. We would've lost everything we built here. I thought, no, since we waited all those years, we can wait even more until we are all citizens. More generally, I was also afraid of how the atmosphere would change after such a decision.

Jamal's journey to America is typical of more recent immigrants, but as in the Middle East itself, Arab-Americans come from diverse backgrounds, religions, and socioeconomic situations. While I was in Chicago, I attended a reception by the American Middle East Voters Alliance, a political action committee. Many Arab-Americans I spoke to there identified themselves not by their country of origin in the Middle East or by their religion, but by the fact that they were equally Arab and American. Many of those attending were judges, lawyers, and doctors, first-, second-, and third-generation immigrants.

The action committee was set up because its members felt an obligation to influence aldermen or district representatives to adopt resolutions condemning ethnic hate speech, hate violence, 'travel bans,' and registration of persons based on ethnicity or religion. The first speaker at the reception was Robert Abood, a third-generation Christian Lebanese-American and a former Democratic nominee for Illinois' 16th Congressional District of the United States House of Representatives. He outlined the main accomplishments of the alliance.

That evening, however, the committee was honouring the 49th District Alderman Joe Moore for his commitment to the Arab-American community and for being chief sponsor of a resolution condemning the president's 'travel ban'. Moore's district is diverse and includes large Arab and Muslim populations. 'These are not ordinary times,' said the alderman during his speech, referring to President Trump's executive order:

> This isn't just about advancing your economic and cultural interests, this is about preserving values. It's contrary to what I was raised to believe, what America was: a tolerant nation, a nation that believes in diversity, a nation that believed in everyone trying to achieve the American dream, of making sure that their children have a better life than they experienced. Those values are under threat in this day and age. It is so important to get your community to organize, raise money, and most importantly get members of your community out to vote. Voting equals influence. People who vote have the power.

A few days after I first met Jamal at Al Bawadi Grill, I called him to arrange another meeting. For three months he had been studying for his citizenship interview, which was scheduled on the following day, 14 May 2017. On the day, he could hardly contain his joy. 'I passed and I cannot describe my happiness,' he told me on the phone. 'This is the moment I have been waiting for all my life.' Faten, who is a permanent resident, was waiting for her interview as well. The couple expected it would take around six more months.

I met the family, who were fasting for Ramadan, outside their home. On several occasions, the couple mentioned that they wanted to show me a park not far from their home in Worth, Illinois. The 'park' is in fact a scenic water reclamation area, with a canal, waterways, waterfalls, ducks, bridges, and a golf course. Jamal drove us there. The children ran after the ducks and balanced on curbs or short uphill passages. Faten told me that life in America had made her a stronger and more independent person.

'Do you feel that Americans view you differently, or feel any sense of discrimination?' I asked.

'I have never felt that,' answered Jamal.

'Yes, on a few occasions,' said Faten. 'When I'm wearing the hijab, people sometimes look at me.'

'Do they just look or do they say anything?' I asked.

'Once a guy and a girl laughed at me and mockingly said "Assalamu alaikum" to me'—a traditional Islamic greeting meaning 'peace be upon you' in Arabic.

'Where was that?'

'It was down the road from my home, where I pick up the kids, but I didn't say anything back. I just prayed for God to guide them on the right path.'

'So this was the only incident?'

'There are a few women at the shopping centre whom I don't like.'

'Why? What do they do?' I asked.

'Sometimes they just stare,' Faten said. 'And sometimes, there is a lady who doesn't want me to pay at her aisle. So I began avoiding her.'

'You told me about a couple of incidents only. Would you say these incidents are rare?'

'Yes. What's nice about Americans here is that you feel that they always smile,' Faten said, smiling widely to demonstrate. 'They smile from here to here, unlike us Arabs, we're always frowning. They wish you a good morning without even knowing who you are.'

In the distance, surrounded by greenery, Jamal chased after his children, occasionally bursting into laughter as he caught up with them. 'When we come here, we forget about any hardship,' said Jamal. 'Never in my life have I seen so many trees, so much grass. It's beautiful. It makes us happy.'

BETWIXT AND BETWEEN: JAMAL SHULTAF

As we were driving back, Jamal and his family took me on a tour of their neighbourhood: the fire station, a children's playground, and their school.

You know the past two years Faten and I have been dreaming about having our own home with a garden. I think we are nearly there. As soon as she and the kids receive their citizenship, we are going make it happen. This, as they say, is the American dream, right?

10

MATERNAL FOREVER

SAWSAN MAANI

Sawsan slammed her silver car door and quickly stepped onto the lime pebble stones half buried under a pile of soil. The sun was bright; a soft wind drew dust from pine trees nearby; traffic clogged the roads. She walked toward me, and suddenly said, 'It gets to a point where I ask myself, where am I in all of this?'

Slim with light ash brown hair, Sawsan Maani is the mother of eight children. The fifty-one-year-old's youngest grandson, Saif, was born on 30 March 2017, a month after our first meeting. Sawsan embodies a lifestyle common to many Jordanian women that focuses solely on being a homemaker, having children and raising them.

Gender roles in Jordan, as in many Arab countries, are dictated through socialization in the family. This is key when it comes to perceptions of women in society and continues to have an impact on their role in their communities today. Arguably, the lack of equality is the result of traditional gender roles and deeply enshrined patriarchal notions.

In some cases, rising prices and a lack of adequate economic means in the family have forced women to find work outside the home to support their husbands, resulting in a balance shift. The country has seen a rise in women leaders—judges, parliamentarians, senators, activists, community leaders—but tribal and religious structures continue to endorse strict gender roles, thwarting women's accession to roles outside the family.

Jordan has one of the highest rates of university-educated women in the Middle East but one of the region's lowest participation rates for women in the labour force, defined in a 2005 World Bank report on gender assessment as the 'social gender paradox'. Lack of social services, particularly nurseries in the private sector, remains a major barrier to educated women returning to work, exacerbated by their socially dictated roles and responsibilities.

Sawsan, whose family originally hails from the southern city of Maan, was raised in Kuwait. Growing up, she adored her wise and affectionate grandmother who belonged to the Circassian minority, the indigenous population of Circassia, a historical region that stretched along the northeast coast of the Black Sea at the border of Europe and Asia. The Circassians were dispersed across the Middle East in the nineteenth century after their defeat at the hands of the Russians when they conquered the Caucasus. They are among the first populations to settle in Jordan and have played a major role in the country's development, holding security and government positions. In 1921, they became the royal guards of King Abdullah I, the founder of modern Jordan.

Sawsan's father worked at a petroleum company in Kuwait. As an expatriate family, they lived a sheltered life with playgrounds, private schools, bicycles, and swimming pools. They hardly ever met Kuwaitis, and every summer they flocked back to Amman to escape the excruciating heat and humidity.

In school, Sawsan loved French class, so much so that she immersed herself in the language by taking private lessons and later enrolling at a French institute. Her parents, who still lived in Kuwait at the time, encouraged her to attend university and sent her back to Jordan. She wanted to become a journalist, but arguments with a faculty member at the university department led her to switch her major to history.

'I wasn't thinking of marriage at all,' she told me. 'Just like any other student, I was thinking about working, especially since my family is open-minded. We're not backwards, thank God, so my plan was to graduate, work, see where life takes me. I had a lot of ambition.'

Three years later, while still attending university, she was married. Her family had moved back to Jordan after she completed her first year at the university. Her mother's female friends had begun seeking wives for their sons, and the plan was to include Sawsan. The women visited each other at home and exchanged information about their children's characteristics and traits. Sawsan, twenty-two years old at the time, knew nothing of this until she returned home from university one day and her mother told her what was going on. She was surprised that any member of her family had considered marrying her off, and she told her mother it was too soon.

> I was in a daze. I couldn't grasp what was going on. My mum wanted to make sure I was okay, but that doesn't mean that I had to get married to someone from her friend's side. She didn't force it on me. She told me to just meet him, and that if I felt okay about it we would go ahead, and if not, we wouldn't. So I said okay. I agreed to meet the man and we sat together. I couldn't decide how I felt about him. I was too focused on the whole arrangement, but slowly I began focusing on him more. He was composed, he was mature, he was smart, he was wise. Still, we barely met with each other before the engagement. My father was travelling and until it was official, we weren't really talking a lot, I couldn't be with him properly.

Sawsan and her parents' only prerequisite was that she continue her final semester at university after marriage, which she did. Sawsan and Ahmad Jaber were married on 4 August 1989, and only a few months later she became pregnant with identical twin girls, Hiba and Hadeel. Even after the twins were born, the young mother still had work on her mind. When she went out, friends and relatives encouraged her to work. She sent her CV to companies and corporations, but when she returned home she pondered on her choices, concluding, 'No, I can't do this.' It was impossible for her to imagine the girls in anyone else's care, especially when the couple had a third daughter, Nada, whose name means 'dew' in Arabic, just one year later. 'They were the only thing on my mind. I forgot about working.'

In 1994, the family moved to a neighbourhood south of Amman called Marj Al-Hamam, or Meadow of the Doves. Back then, vast wheat fields crowned the hilltops and only three other homes had been built. They did not even have electricity. Today, the fields have been swallowed by homes, electric cables weave across pylons, and the only remaining hint of wheat is found in the small plot of land sandwiched between two houses. Down the street from her home, there is a small neighbourhood grocery shop, with a red sign and a fridge filled with ice cream tucked between the entrance and the pavement. Countless other shops, bakeries, clothing stores, and fitness centres are nearby. Roads and bridges today connect Marj Al-Hamam to the centre of Amman.

> In ten years, the entire area has transformed. You can look outside, we are surrounded now by homes and the wheat fields are gone. It happened in a flash, the buildings, the towers, the shops. I mean, we used to source our electricity from a stone factory here. I think it still exists. The whole neighbourhood used electricity from there. You can't imagine how it was.

> For a period, I felt there was no life in this place. I thought, 'I can't live here any longer.' My husband would go to work, he's a banker, and I would be here on my own with the girls, and they were all so young. It was difficult and sometimes we just had one car. I felt I was

stranded. I would look out and see all the streets empty. After sunset, everything was pitch dark. I would just sit and wait until my husband came home, and sometimes he had to work late.

The first time I met Sawsan, she was wearing a white jumper, jeans, and brown boots with wide heels. She insisted we meet at a café her daughters had recommended. It was unlit with tinted windows and loud music, tucked behind a noisy road in Amman next to an empty car park and office buildings. Young men and women whiled away the late-afternoon hours, drinking ice-blended lemonade with mint and smoking *argeeleh*.

When Sawsan had said she was searching for herself as she slammed the car door, I realized that having time for herself was rare. By the time our first meeting ended, it was already dark outside. A few families and couples came and went, but it was mainly young men. She talked, laughed, and cried—twice. Sawsan drank coffee, then ordered lemonade with mint. 'Please have something, maybe more tea?' she asked, as if we were sitting in her own home. At times, she looked around the café in a daze, as if reflecting, and took sips from her coffee cup with a sense of release.

The only other time she had for herself in that same way was back in the nineties, when her three daughters all attended nursery and she was alone for part of the day. During that period, she had contemplated her family's future, but also her own. Just one more child, she thought, a brother for her three daughters.

Eventually that thought would turn into an obsession. Sawsan prefers to call it a dream, in the sense of being unconscious or sleep-walking. Although the patriarchal mindset remains a predominant reality in Jordan, Ahmad insisted he was happy with his family at the time and did not necessarily want more children. He told me when we met later that he did not care what other people thought or said. 'I'm also neither king nor rich,' he mused. 'I don't need an heir, and to pass on what? I don't say this because they are my daughters but they were more than enough for me, they are wonderful.'

Sawsan wanted to believe she did not care either, but one incident incensed her. 'I was thinking, no matter what people say, it doesn't make a difference. But no, it does.' Sawsan was out shopping with her three daughters one day and was carrying two of her children. The family's housekeeper was carrying the third. As Sawsan approached her car to open the door, a couple of elderly women who were waiting for a taxi came up to her. One of them asked her if they were all her daughters, she recalled.

> One woman said, 'May God bless them. Don't you have a son? Poor you.' These words really tore me apart inside. I mean, why poor me? In our family, we didn't have that mindset, favouring boys over girls. I don't know if it's ignorance or what, but eventually words do get to you. Wherever I went, I would hear, 'Poor you, poor you, what a pity.' Why? Whenever I tried to forget about this issue, they reminded me. I would sometimes cry. I would think, 'Leave me alone.' I'm the kind of person who doesn't like to appear weak or defeated, so I always behaved as if it didn't matter, and it really didn't, but when I faced the same thing everywhere I went, even when it was indirect, even when it was told out of love, it hurt me.

Ahmad suggested the couple take a vacation—his wife was exhausted. They went to Turkey and left their children with their parents. It was time for reflection as well. She felt grateful for her marriage and her children, she said, but also wondered if she would be able to work or fulfil any of the ambitions that she had once had, to immerse herself once again in French, or to become a journalist.

The desire, however, to have a son took over her life. Nearly every two years after that, Sawsan had a baby. After having her third daughter, she began reading about medical advancements, and wondered about ways to guarantee that her next baby would be a boy. She visited several doctors, had several procedures done, and took injections. But when she next became pregnant, she miscarried in her third month. It was a boy. Knowing that gave her an incentive to try again.

Hayat, a fourth daughter and whose name means 'life', was born in 1994, shortly before the family moved to Marj Al-Hamam. Her mother was not sad, but rather angry that she was not a boy. Sawsan was surprised at the way she was becoming. 'I reached a stage where all I wanted was a son,' she explained. 'It was like I was being stubborn against my fate. It was wrong. Such an obsession ended up having a great influence on my entire life.'

Sawsan is serious, organized and disciplined. She is hard on herself. Confirming this, Hayat later described her mother as wanting her house to be 'perfect'. She still does most of the housework and cooks every meal. Growing up, the four daughters had a strict routine, determining when they ate, when they dressed, when they slept. It was a routine Sawsan enforced on all her children. Otherwise, she said, 'everything around me would have collapsed with eight kids.'

Her need to be in control sometimes led to tensions in her home. If she didn't manage to cook for some reason, she became upset. Ahmad would tell her, 'We won't die from hunger, we can order something.' She worried too much, organized too much, cared too much. Her husband, in some ways, was the opposite— laid-back, calm, nonchalant.

After she gave birth to Hayat, Sawsan's mother and husband both told her to give her body a break, but whenever she saw a baby boy anywhere, she still wanted one of her own. She became pregnant again, this time with twin boys, but she had a miscarriage in her first trimester. Physically, she was exhausted; mentally, she was devastated.

I went home and thought, what am I doing to myself? This is God's will. Stop it. That's enough. My husband began to refuse to have more children because of my health. He said, 'I'm happy with what we have. If you're doing this for me, the girls mean the world to me, I don't want a son.' He was very considerate of my feelings. He was supportive.

After the second miscarriage, Sawsan wanted to do something for herself, as she described it, more than 'just giving birth and having kids.' Still, she had to raise her four daughters and manage the house. Ahmad often worked long hours at the bank and if she had wanted to work full-time, he would have been unable to manage the household.

Sawsan decided to open her own shop, to be, as she described it, 'my own boss.' Her parents owned a single-story house with a separate entrance to the garage. She used the entrance to open a small grocery shop and her family helped her obtain a licence. Ahmad worried about her supervising the shop all day. Friends and family members told her she wouldn't be able to manage, but for a while, she proved them wrong.

I would go and ask where the wholesale stores were to buy merchandise. I wanted to sell and be competitive. I couldn't buy the goods from other competing supermarkets. So I asked around and would go by car and load the merchandise and display it. Even though we didn't need this financially, I enjoyed the work. It was a joy. My husband said, why are you doing this? I was like, why not? There's nothing shameful about it. It's not a shame to work. I didn't have anything to be ashamed of. I didn't care what anybody thought. All I cared about was me. I mean it wasn't just work. On the contrary, I was helping people in the neighbourhood. They were happy it was there. People would say, Sawsan, you really are doing this. It was amazing. I would even travel by car to Syria to buy merchandise from there.

She named the store Tasahul or 'convenience' in Arabic. She bought items that were in demand. On one occasion, an elderly lady came to the shop searching for dried okra. Sawsan went out, found some, and sold it to her. Children often came and asked for coloured cotton candy, and when Sawsan could not find it in Jordan, she travelled to Damascus and purchased it along with sugar-covered sweets. The profit was negligible, but Sawsan felt happy. At the time, larger supermarkets, like Cozmo, an upscale shopping centre, did not exist. Safeway was considered too far away for her customers. Sawsan targeted housewives and children returning from school. Her shop's asset was true to its name: convenient.

Opening a small grocery shop wasn't what Sawsan had always aspired to do as a career, she admitted, but it was what she had to do for her own self-worth. To her surprise, when she was working, she was also more organized in her life, even at home. All of her daughters asked her how she managed the shop and her house, recalled Sawsan. 'They still say, "Mum, we can't handle one baby, how did you manage with all of us?"' She is honest with them. She tells them that she doesn't have an answer. 'I have a rule though,' she told me. 'If you are organized in your life, then everything will be easier. I tell my girls, "Be organized when it comes to your children's food, drink, tidying up your house, your appointments. Organization is the basis of life."'

Every pregnancy after Hayat was planned. In 1996, Dalal, their fifth daughter, was born. Although Sawsan asked the doctor not to inform her of the baby's gender, her doctor performed an invasive procedure, including in vitro fertilization for gender selection, and guaranteed it would be a boy. When Dalal was born and they returned home, Sawsan said there was no time to be upset, or depressed. Meanwhile, Ahmad, whom Sawsan described as someone who 'built himself from scratch', was working hard and as the family grew, so did the financial difficulties. There were the costs of school tuition, activities and maintaining the household. 'Despite all of this, my husband is generous, he doesn't care a great deal about saving money. I would push him to save and to think of the future.' Although three of his daughters are today relatively financially independent, Ahmad often has three of his children attending university at the same time, with mounting tuition fees.

Sawsan had been busy raising her daughters, managing the supermarket and preparing to move into her new home in Marj Al-Hamam. She was overwhelmed, she admitted, and eventually rented out the supermarket. Still, when she had settled in to her new home, she began contemplating having a son again.

Instead, Diala, a sixth daughter, was born shortly after her fifth. Perhaps, she said, she had used all her chances. For eight years, she did not have any more children. She felt she no longer had the same urge to have a boy and she was barely managing her household: cleaning, cooking, repairing, shopping, helping with homework, driving to after-school activities.

Then, in 2003, she thought to herself, 'seventh time lucky.' She became pregnant, and when she visited a doctor in her second trimester, he told her it was a boy. 'I was thrilled,' she recalled. 'I was on cloud nine. My mother bought me a whole bag filled with stuff for a baby boy.' In fact, she was pregnant with another girl. During her last trimester, she went with Ahmad to the doctor, who told her everything was fine, but asked for her husband's phone number instead of hers.

> My husband and I looked at each other and the doctor seemed anxious. So my husband asked him, 'What's wrong? Is there something wrong with the baby?' He assured us, 'No, everything is fine. Don't worry. The baby is in good health. I just need Ahmad's phone number.' At that moment, I knew, or felt it right away. I knew it was a girl. I tried to deny it but I couldn't. There was a moment where I didn't want to hear it. I didn't want to know.

> I was anxious. When he called, I handed the phone to my husband and stood far away. I heard my husband say, 'No, you couldn't have done anything about it, this is God's will. Thank God. What matters

is that the baby is healthy. Everything is fine. We're thankful for whatever God sends us.' I should have given more thought to what I was undertaking and thought about what I was doing but I was extremely stubborn when it came to this issue. In the end, it was me who pushed my husband. He would say, no, that's enough, this is draining you. I would say, for God's sake, please do this for me. He would agree, just to please me. He would swear that it didn't matter to him but I would become upset when they called him 'Abu Hiba', or father of Hiba. All his friends had sons.

The parents called their seventh daughter Farah, or 'happiness'. 'She was an amazing baby,' said Sawsan. 'She was beautiful.' Although convinced her chances of bearing a boy were running out, she clung to the remotest of hopes that she might yet have a son. I asked her how she could believe any of the doctors after all of this. 'When someone wants something, they have a little extra hope,' she explained. This time, though, it was a doctor she had not previously met who convinced her to try having a boy one more time.

When she went to the clinic, she found the women there all had sons. Sawsan cried and told the senior doctor at the time she could not go through another pregnancy and that her body was tired. The doctor performed medical tests, and informed her that her body was in good condition. She felt hopeful, and considered going through the procedure one more time.

Still, she had to persuade Ahmad. She had to plead with him. He reminded her of the times they had tried, and that if it was meant to be, it would have happened. 'I was like a child, clinging to hope, and I was ready to do anything to persuade him.' Ahmad was worried about her health as well. When I met him at their home, and Sawsan went to the kitchen to bring juice, he confessed that every time she became pregnant, 'my heart would sink to the ground and remain heavy for nine months. I just wanted them to be healthy, that's all, and in the end, it was her wish. She wanted a boy.'

Sawsan felt guilty, mainly for the financial burdens she was imposing on her husband by bringing yet another child into their family. They were forced to move their seven daughters from private to public school, because they could no longer afford the tuition fees. Sawsan still had a house to manage, but she also began working from home. She bought dresses and clothing items from Syria and sold them to people she knew and their friends. The profits were meagre, but Sawsan said she enjoyed it.

When she was in her second trimester, she developed severe back pain and spent a month bedridden. She visited her doctor who performed an ultrasound. He told her the chances of the baby being a boy were high, but he would not guarantee it. 'He said 90 per cent, I wanted 120 per cent,' said Sawsan. She stopped going to the doctor altogether, until the ninth month of her pregnancy. The doctor told her the baby was developed and she was ready for delivery. She was only two weeks shy of her due date and the doctor told her he could give her a pill to speed up the process. Sawsan refused; she felt anxious.

> We left the doctor's office and my husband said, 'Why not just give birth and get it over with?' I said I didn't want to. He said, 'What do you mean you don't want to? Sooner or later you're going to deliver this baby. This baby is coming, what's the point of still worrying whether it's a boy or girl?' His voice was getting louder and he was becoming angry. He said, 'Give yourself a break.' Then it dawned on me: I was going to have another baby. I was going to be happy if I had a son, but then I thought, what have I done? Eight children? I didn't say this to Ahmad. I just told him, 'Please take me to the market. I want to walk. I might take the pill, and I need to fix the house, I need to cook.' He said, 'You're about to give birth and you want to cook and fix the house?'

It was one of the few times in their marriage that Ahmad raised his voice in anger. She went back and took the pill; there was no turning back. While at the hospital, the doctors rushed her in and performed a caesarean section. At forty-one years old, on 27 October 2007, Sawsan finally give birth to a son, Abdullah.

A few weeks after our first meeting, Sawsan invited me to her home. She met me outside, wearing jeans, a white and baby blue jumper with light pink flowers, and a gold flower pendant. We entered a small gate next to a rectangular patch of grass and short trees. The empty plot of land near their home was filled with half-grown wheat and shrubs but was mainly covered with dark soil. The rest of her neighbourhood was lined with white stone homes, most of which displayed black and white steel bars across the windows. Three outdoor steps led to an open door where Ahmad and nine-year-old Abdullah greeted us, shaking my hand warmly. We spoke briefly before Ahmad announced he was taking his son, who was wearing his white uniform and green belt, to Taekwondo class. As he was leaving, Abdullah proudly told me that his older sister, Farah, had a black belt, denoting her skill and higher ranking.

Sawsan smiled politely and led me inside to the salon, an area in the house reserved mainly for guests. A small statue of the renowned Egyptian singer Umm Kulthum took pride of place atop a display cabinet. The ceramic statue has the singer carrying her famous signature cloth tissue in her hands and her band seated in a semi-circle behind her. Two side lamps with deer-skin shades, bought at a bazaar in Amman, cast a soft light. As we sat on maroon red sofas, Sawsan explained that she found comfort in shopping and decorating her house.

My hostess brought out homemade lemonade with savoury Syrian pastries covered in cheese. A dark chocolate cake covered in frosting sat next to a silver tray that had been set with ginseng tea, lemon and ginger tea, cappuccino packets, and Nescafé. Sawsan poured the tea into pretty white and gold teacups, and invited Hayat to join us. Like her mother, Hayat is slim with brown hair hanging just below her neck, and she wore a necklace with an angel pendant. As Sawsan sliced the cake, both mother and daughter confessed they ate desserts nearly every day. Sawsan preferred to bake them herself rather than buy them from a bakery.

Hayat spoke about her semester in Turkey, before she had graduated from the University of Jordan, and about how time away from her crowded family had changed her life. 'What I want in life is to be independent,' she mused, toying with her pendant. 'When I'm searching for a job, I won't be required to leave it someday because of my home or my husband. I want to be able to make choices.'

'I tell my girls they shouldn't choose the path I did,' Sawsan admitted.

Today, Sawsan values what little free time she has, and finds it right before she goes to bed. She sits with her smartphone and *argeeleh*; her husband drinks a cup of coffee and smokes a cigarette. They reflect, and sometimes she writes down her thoughts. Hayat shares her thoughts on Instagram; her mother does the same on Facebook. In 2013, Sawsan posted on Facebook:

Dignity, pride, then me. The time for tears is over. Live far from people's illusions.

Unlike her mother, Hayat said she would like to have a small family one day. 'In a way, I am only now learning who my mother is as a person because when we were growing up, when there are eight kids, there was no time, she could only be a mum, trying to do everything she did.'

Abdullah returned from Taekwondo, and dashed in and out of the salon. He offered me a piece of chewing gum. Then he scampered out before returning to show me his PlayStation games: The Lego Movie, FIFA. Hayat often helps him with his homework, and Farah plays sports with him. Being not only the youngest but also the only boy, Abdullah gets the most attention, but is the only one of the children to have given his parents

a hard time at school, refusing to do his homework and performing poorly in his classes. His parents twice moved him to different schools, but now feel he has finally settled. I asked him when
his birthday was. 'In October,' he replied excitedly. 'Why don't
you come to my birthday party?'

Sawsan used to imagine that as her children grew up, the
burden of parenting would lighten, that they would be able to
depend more on themselves. As they continue to grow older, she
explained, the responsibilities have increased. With two of her
children still in school, and her daughters relying on her after
their own children were born, Sawsan realizes she will seldom
ever get the break she yearns for.

> You begin dealing with different personalities. I have to deal with
> seven or eight different personalities. Each one of them has a mind
> of her own. I must care for each one of them, pamper each one,
> sympathize, be close to the girls. You have to hear them out, you
> have to sit with them, you have to listen to their problems. I was
> well known at their school; I am still known as the mother of the
> Jaber girls.

Still, a few months later Sawsan called me to tell me she was
travelling alone to Beirut to visit a childhood friend. She also sent
me a message asking if we could meet, just the two of us, for a cup
of coffee in Rainbow Street when she returned. We met at a café
overlooking the historical Amman Citadel, the site of the temple
of Hercules. Her daughters insisted they join us as well.

EPILOGUE

Hope is perhaps the most powerful commodity in the Middle East. Around 82 per cent of Syrian refugees in Jordan are now living below the poverty line, including Amal and her family. Despite the prospect of alienation and uncertainty, she has become more resigned to the idea of resettling in Canada to seek a better life. In 2018, the literacy program she dedicated her mornings to ended abruptly and she lost her job. The shoe store where Farhan, her husband, worked closed down.

Jordan's efforts to modernize its economy will face many obstacles, including the staggering rate of female unemployment and the widespread belief that corruption is rampant. Slow economic growth has coincided with a decline in foreign private investment. In the middle of 2018, I saw the largest protests on the streets of Amman since the ill-fated Arab Spring. They were sparked by the introduction of a controversial tax bill and fuelled by long-term issues such as youth unemployment, lack of genuine political participation, and social exclusion. The protests were a sign that fear is slowly being replaced by hope. The demonstrations were an expression of both frustration and a desire for a better future.

The first time I really spoke to Omar Al-Abdallat, the cartoonist, was at a café tucked between large, white stone houses in the capital, Amman. He seemed to be in a reflective mood, as he sipped slowly from a cup of green tea on that rainy evening in December 2016. He was describing a new character he was creating, Sehes—eager, underemployed and educated.

Indeed, I saw Sehes everywhere at the protests—young men, most of them wearing blue jeans, their hair gelled back, chins and cheeks covered in stubble. It was clear a desire for change persisted and the fear that plagued them for years after the Arab Spring was dissipating.

Ordinary citizens are largely absent from the debates shaping the present and future of the Middle East. By entering the living rooms of ten ordinary people living in Jordan, this book offers an insight into their everyday lives—their struggles, their dreams and their perspectives on the region's deeper problems. They reflect society and the complex political identity of Jordan.

The current circumstances will most likely see Jordan remaining dependent on foreign aid for economic and financial stability. This comes at a price, of course, including more regional and international concessions. During a televised interview in July 2018, Wafa Bani Mustafa, the parliamentarian featured in this book, referred to the concessions as 'blackmailing'. In other words, they dictate the country's foreign policy.

Indeed, dynamics in the Middle East are changing. Saudi Arabia's strategic shift to align itself with Israel and the current American administration to counter Iran may lead Jordan's role as a regional mediator to become less vital. Despite its reservations about a final Palestinian–Israeli peace deal and the United States' recognition of Jerusalem as the capital of Israel, Jordan's government remains in a delicate position due to its heavy dependence on American aid. The peace deal is perceived by many Jordanians as benefitting only Israel and sidelining Palestinians and Jordanians, both of whom have a big stake in the settlement's outcome.

One of the most striking features of the region, including Jordan, is its share of youth. Millennials like Fayez, Naser

Farhan's son, make up nearly half of Jordan's population. Many of them are looking for jobs. The first time I met Fayez, he was eighteen years old, standing in a wide black cell. He was accused of promoting the Islamic State, or ISIS. Today, he is twenty-three years old and reflective. 'When you saw me in court, I thought I knew everything to know about life,' he explained when we met in 2018. 'I know there's so much more to learn. I can't judge people because of their beliefs or the way they look. I judge people based on their actions and their kindness.'

If I learned anything from my work on this book, it was that Fayez is the product of his environment. His hometown Russeifeh hardly offers hope. In early 2018, floor cracks in Naser's home led to its complete collapse. The family moved to a nearby apartment that has a bare, incomplete steep staircase. Fayez can't find work, in the public or private sector, because of a prerequisite need for security clearance. For the foreseeable future, he will probably continue working in menial jobs. 'Even when someone like me wants to change,' Fayez told me in Amman one warm summer afternoon, 'the forces seem to be against you.'

Still, Fayez sees hope in his smartphone. He watches historical documentaries to understand the world and National Geographic videos to learn about other people and places. Like his brother Mustafa, he dreams of leaving Russeifeh. It is not only poverty or illiteracy or a skewed view of religion that is driving youth to extremism, but rather marginalization, and, increasingly, a lack of trust in the government.

If young people continue to face a sense of hopelessness in their future and find no opportunities for personal and professional development, including once they are released from prison, they will continue to be vulnerable to misconceived narratives and ideologies. They will seek after power and control, wherever those may be. Therefore, it is important for them to feel engaged. The government cannot combat extremism or other social ills if it lacks credibility.

Recently I reread an article I wrote at the beginning of the Arab Spring, more than seven years ago. Back then, Jordanians were holding strikes and protesting in the streets, calling for transparency, accountability, and better economic policies. In that same article, I refer to yet another missed opportunity for comprehensive reform in 2004 when a national agenda reform was drafted and presented to the government, only to be shelved shortly after.

Change was promised again after the June 2018 protests. Without serious reform in the electoral laws, more civil rights, and better economic policies, we will continue to be challenged. Reacting to the 2018 protests, King Abdullah tried to head off anger by siding with the demonstrators. In a sharp rebuke, the king even accused most of his ministers of being asleep. It wasn't the first time he had done so, nor the first time he had sacked a prime minister—the new leader is the seventh prime minister since 2011. The king appoints governments, approves legislation, and can dissolve parliament. During the Arab Spring, there were promises by King Abdullah to consult parliament in choosing a new prime minister. Gradually, it became evident this would not materialize, revealing yet again the flaws of the Jordanian electoral system.

For a younger generation reared on the internet, like Lina Assad, who is entering her last year in high school, and Sultan, the young soldier in Wadi Rum, change is no longer a question of political will, but a matter of when. They see the region, they see the world, and feel like there's no turning back. Yet, Syria offers a sombre reminder that hope ebbs and flows. The international community and Arab countries have allowed Syria's ruler Bashar al-Assad to remain in power despite the devastation and carnage his regime has wreaked. For Jordan's government—and for the country's drivers and merchants, whose businesses were crippled by the closure of the border with Syria—the Assad regime regaining the upper hand in the war might mean the reopening of the border crossing, which could boost Jordan's flailing economy by allowing commerce to flow once again. For some villages in northern Jordan, cross-border trade was their only lifeline.

Yet, the Assad regime's longevity also means the main motivating factors for the protests in Syria during the Arab Spring—fear, lack of freedom, human rights abuses, including torture—will continue. This has driven many of the refugees in Jordan with whom I have spoken to seek hope elsewhere. What does the future hold for the Syrian people?

As for Jordan, it has survived as a rentier state but it was never really viable or sustainable. Sustainability means implementing practical political and social policies and programmes. In Jordan too, the underlying conditions behind the desire for change persist. Since 2011, public debates have been repressed or even banned in Jordan. Suspensions and detentions of student activists have continued. Fear and self-censorship have returned. This is no longer an approach that Jordan can afford. The message of the 2018 protests is that something will have to give.

The lack of confidence and trust between the people and the government cannot be overcome except through a model of political reform that offers to bridge the gap between an angry public and a distant, ineffective system of government. In order to change the current economic model, Jordan's relationship between the state and the people needs to change, through reforms that build trust and allow the people to buy into the political structure. Jordan needs to nurture strong political parties that encourage youth engagement in politics. Citizens need to be empowered; the people of Jordan want their voices to be heard.